For Leslie

Kindred Spirit

SPIRIT

William Edelen

love & light

Bill Edelen

"The spirit of man is nomad, his blood bedouin, and love is the aboriginal tracker on the faded desert spoor of his lost self: and so I came to live my life not by conscious plan or prearranged design but as someone following the flight of a bird."

— Laurens van der Post

JOSLYN-MORRIS, Publishers
1647 Federal Way
Boise, Idaho 83707

ABOUT THE AUTHOR

William Edelen was born in West Texas and spent his boyhood there and in Oklahoma City. He flew for twelve years as a U.S. Marine Corps pilot, flying both fighter planes and transports in World War II and Korea. This included one tour of duty as one of five personal pilots assigned to the staff of the Commandant of the Marine Corps, Washington, D.C. He requested a discharge and returned to Oklahoma State University where he received the Bachelor of Science degree in Horticulture. He then entered McCormick Theological Seminary (on the campus of the University of Chicago) where he received his Masters degree in Theology.

After serving Presbyterian churches for six years he received a grant to do further studies in the Graduate School of Anthropology, the University of Colorado. Concluding two years there he returned to the active ministry in the Congregational Church. He taught Comparative Religion and Anthropology for seven years at the University of Puget Sound in Tacoma, Washington. During those same years he was the minister of the First Congregational Church in Tacoma.

Since 1981 he has been the minister of the Community Congregational Church in the resort town of McCall, Idaho. He is a regular columnist for *The Idaho Statesman* of Boise, Idaho, *The Herald*, of Everett, Washington, and the *Press Democrat* of Santa Rosa, California. His first book of columns, *Toward the Mystery*, published in 1983, was chosen by the National Methodist Women's organization as one of their study books for 1986.

For . . . all of the supportive spirits
in the Community Congregational
Church of McCall, Idaho

Betty and Glenn Mapes
of Allenspark, Colorado

and all of those kindred spirits . . .
everywhere . . . who even though
invisible to one another . . . belong
to that mystical community . . .
where spirits touch and light the
darkness . . . as candle flames in the night . . .

ABOUT THE COVER

by
Elizabeth (Jerry) Edelen

The clear and fine day and the walk around Redfish Lake in the Sawtooth mountains of Idaho remain in my mind's eye. As I climbed higher along the golden trail I asked the mother and grandmother spirits for help in visualizing the pattern of a rug that I wanted to begin.

An inner vision came of circles within circles and the wonderous symmetry between the eastern God (Tao) and the Wakan-Tanka of the Sioux Indians.

There is in both concepts the belief not in a Creator, but in Creativity, a universal energy found everywhere in everything. The circle in the Eastern view represented heaven; the Tai Chi disk symbolized the wholeness found in complimentary opposites and the cyclic system of perpetual becoming. Black and white, male and female, growth and decay, and the Jungian concept of the shadow self underlying the conscious mind, all balance and inter-relate in a seamless web of movement.

To the Native American the circle represents all things that exist. Black Elk said: "The sky is round and the earth and stars are round. The wind in its greatest power whirls. The sun comes forth and goes down again in a circle. The moon does the same and both are round. The birds fly in a circle and make their nests in a circle, for theirs is the same religion as ours."

O ••• O ••• O ••• O ••• O ••• O ••• O

The rug then has as its center the Tai-Chi disk in red, the color representing the sacred earth, and blue, the heavens. It is surrounded by ten circles (physicists theorize that there are ten dimensions) of Native American designs among which are represented truth, freedom and nature's lessons. The following words from Black Elk are interwoven:

> "Wakan-Tanka, like the circle, has no end.
> He is within all things, trees, grasses, rivers, mountains,
> and all the four legged and winged ones."

V

The buffalo in the rug is the four-legged animal, the eagle is the winged one, the trout are the fish of the waters, and the daisies are the green things of the earth.

The number seven is sacred to the Indians and they perceived that there are seven directions including north (white), south (green) east (yellow) and west (black), then the heavens, the earth, and the seventh being the individual from whom all consciousness extends.

Standing in the center of the circle of the rug, one is reminded of the seven directions, the harmony of all the creation and the sacredness of Wakan-Tanka, the great Mystery within all things.

Photography by Earl Brockman

Grandmother Rug Number One
(HOOKED — 9' DIAMETER)

Introduction

We are living in a time when we are inundated, through television, radio and magazines, by the fundamentalist, evangelical, "born again" religious voice. These columns, and this book, offer an intelligent alternative, another option. I have lost count of the letters that have said: "Thank you for bringing in so much fresh air. How refreshing it is to hear a minister speak to the questions that I have always asked . . . and everyone avoided." One woman wrote: "In high school I asked my minister to explain the Trinity. I told him it made no sense at all to me. He just patted me on the head, in a condescending way, and said, 'Some day, when you are grown you will understand it.' Well. I am grown and I still do not understand it." This letter from an Idaho Lutheran minister: "Thank you for helping some of us ministers come out of the closet and discuss things from the pulpit that we have been afraid to face."

These columns have been written for minds that are not afraid to question, and for those free spirits who realize that religious beliefs can be examined by the same critical and objective eye as any other belief system. If you feel that Christianity, and religion is saturated still with witchcraft, magic and superstition, then you will receive much from this book. It is my firm belief that religious creeds and dogma have no place in the world we live in. They are a violation to the free mind and spirit of human beings.

"I have sworn upon the altar of God eternal hostility against every form of tyranny over the mind of man" wrote Thomas Jefferson. No tyranny can so bind human minds in chains as religious tyranny. This book of columns is for those brave enough to examine the chains. The reward for such an examination is freedom, freedom to pursue the religious quest in your own way, guided only by your own insights, your own feelings and your very own intuition, as you point your life toward the Source . . . and toward . . . the Mystery . . . with Spirit as your guide. Since my first book of columns, *Toward the Mystery*, the invitations that have come to me to speak, lecture, lead seminars, appear on radio and television shows, and the response to those appearances indicate to me the hunger that is 'out there' from thousands seeking an intelligent approach to the Mystery in our own time. Spirit . . . will contribute toward filling that need.

William Edelen
at Maka Wakan
in the Moon of the New Grass
McCall, Idaho
1988

"The SPIRIT is not only reason . . . although it includes reason; it is not only feeling . . . but of course it includes feeling as well. It is . . . above all . . . INTUITION . . . which is a profound compass, bearing on our origin and destination. And this is ultimately what religion is all about: 'origin and destination.' The SPIRIT has abandoned the human being in his narrowed, rational state, indulging the greatest pastime and speciality of our time, which is finding first-rate reasons for DOING PARTIAL AND WRONG THINGS."

— Laurens van der Post

Table of Contents

H. THOUGHTS ABOUT MYSTICISM

I. GOD AND THE TAO . . .
EAST AND WEST . . . HOW WE DIFFER

The Dream . . .
Dreaming Us

When I finished this exquisite closing paragraph of *The Labyrinth of Solitude* by Octavio Paz, my eyes were moist.

"Modern man likes to pretend that his thinking is wide awake. But this wide awake thinking has led us into the mazes of a nightmare in which the torture chambers are endlessly repeated in the mirrors of reason. When we emerge, perhaps we will realize that we have been dreaming with our eyes open, and that the dreams of reason are intolerable. And then, perhaps, we will begin to dream once more with our eyes closed."

Behind my closed eyes a dream did begin to take shape. My dream saw Western Christianity, that has now degenerated into hundreds of squabbling, fighting denominations, creeds and sects, evolving toward a higher consciousness and a rediscovery of the sacred, that could lead us out of the maze. The giant barrier standing between us and this rediscovery is the desperate clinging to an archaic, anthropomorphic, supernatural God, "out there" somewhere, watching over us as a divine windowpeeker, or waiting, in the role of a cosmic bellhop.

The sacred is not just a prehistoric stage in the history of human consciousness; it is an element of that consciousness that has been crowded out by the "dreams of reason that are intolerable." Just to live as a human being is a religious and sacred act. The true atheist is not that person who no longer believes in the existence of an anthropomorphic God, but the true atheist is that person *who refuses to recognize the sacredness of existence*, from the very breath of our bodies to the rhythmic ballet of the constellations, and the mystery within those expressions.

What is "religion" without an anthropomorphic, supernatural "God?" What remains of our spiritual quest?

The answer is: EVERYTHING. Sacred reality remains. It would be a way of life founded upon the sacredness of our very existence. It says that the sacred life is life lived in the pursuit of truth. It is life lived in the pursuit of excellence, wisdom and love.

Awareness of the sacred reality of existence includes the sacraments of birth, marriage, reproduction and death. (A sacrament is quite simply a symbol of a sacred and spiritual reality.) Sacred realities include our mental, moral and spiritual growth, the existence of potency of human ideals, dreams and vision. It finds holiness in natural realities that includes not only celestial bodies, rocks, waters and evolving life, but also human beings with body, brain/mind and spirit.

It is daily standing in awe before the unfathomable mystery that dances through electrons and galaxies.

And there is more to living the sacred life: it is to shed over every daily task the light of truth and personal integrity. It is to turn to other members of our species, Homo sapiens, and cast some sunshine on their daily path, to lighten somehow, in some way, their sorrows and give them the joys of affection. It is to blow on the divine spark within their hearts.

"Sometime our light goes out, but is blown again into flame by an encounter with another human being," wrote Albert Schweitzer, and so it is.

Perhaps before it is too late, we will understand that "our dreams of reason have been intolerable" and have led us to "the nightmare of the torture chambers, endlessly repeated." Perhaps, once again, we can "dream, with our eyes closed" and with clear vision see the part that we, you and I, can play in restoring a consciousness of the sacred to our collective memory.

And then, perhaps, yes perhaps, swords will be beat into plow-shares . . . sparrows will not fall to the ground unknown . . . and the least shall finally be considered side by side with the greatest.

AMERICA'S FOUNDING FATHERS

Rejection of Christianity

Who made the following statement? (Choose one.)
"I do not find in orthodox Christianity one redeeming feature."
A. Ronald Keagan
B. Thomas Jefferson
You chose B. Right!

Many of those doing all the bellowing today claim that "humanists" include all those who don't want prayer in public schools, who don't believe that the *Bible* is the "word of God," who don't believe that Jesus was the "son of God," and who don't believe that Christianity is the one "true" religion.

They should read more history. By their definition, our Founding Fathers were unadulterated "humanists" (and that would also include Abraham Lincoln).

The God, the *Bible* and the Jesus of orthodox Christianity was to them an abomination, a scandal and the antithesis of profound and deep spirituality. And yet they all had a very intense private and personal sense of the mystery that we call God. But it was not the orthodox "God," in any sense.

Thomas Jefferson wrote: "Question with boldness the existence of God. I do not believe any of the Christian doctrines. The greatest enemies of Jesus are the doctrines and creeds of the church. It would be more pardonable to believe in no God at all than to blaspheme him by the atrocious writings of the theologians. John Calvin was a demon and malignant spirit." Jefferson wrote that prayer in public schools should be strictly voluntary and always in an area apart from the classroom.

James Madison wrote: "During almost 15 centuries the legal establishment known as Christianity has been on trial, and what have been the fruits, more or less, in all places? These are the fruits: pride, indolence, ignorance and arrogance in the clergy. Ignorance, arrogance and servility in the laity, and in both clergy and laity, superstition, bigotry and persecution."

George Washington refused to take communion. He refused to kneel in church, when he went. He was called "only a Unitarian, if anything" by Episcopalian minister James Abercrombie.

When looking for servants, Washington emphasized that any good person would be fine "be they Mohammedan, Jew, Christian, or atheist." His adopted daughter wrote: "My father was not one of those to act or pray so that he 'might be seen by men.' He communed with his own God in secret."

John Adams left the Congregational Church to become a Unitarian. He wrote: "The 'divinity' of Jesus is made a convenient cover for absurdity. Nowhere in the Gospels do we find a precept for Creeds, Confessions, Oaths, Doctrines and whole carloads of other foolish trumpery that we find Christianity encumbered with."

Abraham Lincoln: "The *Bible* is not my book and Christianity is not my religion. I could never give assent to the long complicated statements of Christian dogma." Lincoln would never be baptized, he would never join a church, he would never make any profession of faith. His own wife said: "My husband is not a Christian but he is a religious man, I think."

My *Webster's New Collegiate Dictionary* defines humanism and humanist very simply as: "The study of the humanities; an attitude of thought centering upon human interests or ideals." That is my definition, too.

Now, for those wanting other definitions: If — and I repeat IF — they claim that "humanists" are those human beings who do not believe in the doctrines and dogma's of orthodox Christianity, and who do not believe that prayer should be in public schools, then it is quite obvious that our great nation was founded by brilliant humanists — and our legacy is humanism.

(Sources are: *In God We Trust,* by Norman Cousins, *George Washington and Religion,* by Paul Boller, *Man and God in Washington,* by Paul Blanshard, The Jefferson-Adams Letters, Thomas Jefferson, edited by Merrill Peterson, *The Complete Madison,* edited by Saul Padover, and *The Autobiography of Benjamin Franklin.*)

Thomas Jefferson and Christianity

Many events will celebrate the 200th anniversary of the Constitution of the United States. In harmony with this historic time, this is the first of a series to explore the religious beliefs of our founding fathers. This topic is very important for two reasons:

■ Very few Americans know what our founding fathers said about Christianity and religion. Recently I did a live radio show in San Francisco on this subject. The telephone calls that came in at the end of the show indicated almost total ignorance of the public on this subject. Most callers wanted to know more.

■ People on the Christian right (the fundamentalists) and the political right continually lie to Americans about the religion of our founding fathers. These men were deeply religious but were not even remotely "Christian."

I am writing in defense of historical accuracy, facts, honesty and integrity, as well as to recover some flavor of the way it really was, rather than how so many fantasize it to be. Too many are like the elderly woman, who when told about evolution replied: "Well, I pray to God that it is not true . . . but if it is true, then I pray to God that nobody ever hears about it." I don't want anyone to say "Oh well, that's just what Bill Edelen thinks they believed," so I will be quoting directly from our founders.

First, they were deists. They did not believe in a personal God, but only in an impersonal force, providence or "nature's God."

Next, they did not believe that the *Bible* was the word of God or sacred literature in any sense. It was just another book. In fact, Thomas Jefferson called it a "dunghill."

What's more, they did not believe that Jesus was in any way divine, or the "son of God." They all found the man-made doctrine of the trinity absurd and comical. They wrote many jokes about it.

When John Kennedy was President, he gave a banquet in the White House that was without precedent. The banquet was for every living American Nobel prize winner, with about 150 present.

At the beginning of the evening, President Kennedy stood and announced that he would make a toast. He said: "Never has so much talent . . . and so much genius . . . been assembled in one room, since Thomas Jefferson dined . . . alone."

Will we ever again see a man or woman of the stature of Jefferson and the other founders in the White House?

The author of the Declaration of Independence, brilliant philosopher, theologian, architect, linguist, statesman, scientist, musician, horticulturist, agronomist, scholar, humanist, deist and master of the civilized arts wrote:

"I have examined all the known superstitions of the world, and I do not find in our particular superstitions of Christianity one redeeming feature. They are all alike, founded on fables and mythology. Millions of innocent men, women and children, since the introduction of Christianity, have been burnt, tortured, fined and imprisoned. What has been the effect of this coercion? To make one half the world fools and the other half hypocrites, to support roguery and error all over the earth."

There is only one piece of sculpture in my study at home. Sitting in the middle of my desk is a magnificent bust of Thomas Jefferson. At the base, it reads: "I have sworn upon the altar of God eternal hostility against every form of tyranny over the mind of man." It is fitting that I begin this series on our Founding Fathers with him.

"Laws and institutions must go hand in hand with the progress of the human mind. As that becomes more developed, more enlightened, as new discoveries are made, new truths disclosed, and manners and opinions change with the change of circumstances, institutions must also advance and keep pace with the times."

— Thomas Jefferson

"I trust that there is not a young person now living in the United States who will not die a Unitarian."

— Ibid

Jefferson's Bible

The Jeffersonian *Bible* became famous and is now in the Smithsonian. Thomas Jefferson literally, took scissors and paste and cut out some of the parables of Jesus that he thought had some ethical value and that was his *Bible*.

He eliminated all of the *Old Testament* because he found it "disgusting" and "degrading." He eliminated the writings of Paul and the rest of the *New Testament* since he found the authors to be "ignorant men."

After cutting out only a few of the teachings of Jesus, he wrote to a friend that he had removed a few "diamonds" from the "dunghill." The *Smithsonian* magazine had an excellent article on the subject a few years ago, noting how he eliminated virgin birth stories, stars in the East, resurrection stories and all other mythology, fables and folklore, which he regarded, in his words, as "rubbish."

There is no doubt as to Jefferson's opinion of Christianity.

Jesus: "The day will come when the mystical generation of Jesus by the Supreme Being as his father, in the womb of a virgin, will be classed with the fable of the generation of Minerva in the brain of Jupiter."

God: "Question with boldness the existence of God; because, if there be one, he will more approve of reason, than of blindfolded fear."

The Trinity: "It is too late in the day for men of sincerity to pretend they believe that three are one . . . and one is three . . . and yet that the one is not three . . . and the three are not one . . . but this constitutes the power and the profits of the priests. Sweep away their gossamer fabrics of fictitious religion and they will catch no more flies."

Christianity: "Christianity has made one half the world fools and the other half hypocrites."

The Clergy: "In every country and in every age, the priest has been hostile to liberty. He is always in alliance with the despot, abetting his abuses in return for protection of his own."

Thomas Jefferson would approve of a recent cartoon from the *Buffalo News*. The cartoon is in four frames. A man is watching the news on his television set.

Frame One: "Oral Roberts came down out of his prayer tower to collect $1.3 million from a dog racing magnate so God wouldn't kill him. The donor said Mr. Roberts wouldn't have to commit suicide now, but did need some psychiatric treatment. Mr. Roberts' son said his dad was 'tickled to death.' More later."

Frame Two: "The Pope announced support for legislation that would cause people who don't want children to have them, and prevent people who do want them and can't from having them."

Frame Three: "Evangelist Jim Bakker said he resigned not because of blackmail over a sex scandal with a church secretary but because of a 'hostile takeover' bid from a rival church. His successor, Jerry Falwell, drew heavy criticism from Bakkers' followers for being a fundamentalist instead of a true charismatic."

Frame Four: "Now, for a report on the movement to get Christian values back into our school classrooms."

The little man down in the corner says: "Time now class, for a pop inquisition."

James Madison on Christianity

"During almost 15 centuries, the legal establishment of Christianity has been on trial. What have been its fruits? These are the fruits, more or less, in all places: pride and indolence in the clergy, ignorance and servility in the laity, and in both clergy and laity, superstition, bigotry and persecution."

James Madison, the father of the Constitution that we are now celebrating, presented this opinion on Christianity to the General Assembly of Virginia in 1785. Madison, our fourth president, continues: "What influence in fact have Christian ecclesiastical establishments had on civil society? In many instances they have been upholding the thrones of political tyranny. In no instance have they been seen as the guardians of the liberties of the people. Rulers who wished to subvert the public liberty have found in the clergy convenient auxiliaries. A just government, instituted to secure and perpetuate liberty, does not need the clergy."

In Virginia, the Episcopal Church was established. In 1744 Christians of all other sects were being arrested and persecuted. Madison addressed that septic situation in these words: "That diabolical, hell conceived, principle of persecution rages; and to their eternal infamy, the clergy can furnish their quota of imps for such a business."

Due to the efforts of Madison and Jefferson, the Episcopal Church was "dis-established" in Virginia. Madison, with all of our Founding Fathers, was adamant in insisting that church and state be separated. He objected to state-supported chaplains in Congress. He objected to the exemption of churches from taxation. And rightly so. They should be taxed.

He wrote: "Religion and government will both exist in greater purity, the less they are mixed together."

The word, "brilliant" is often over-used, but in describing James Madison it is the only word that does this titan justice. James Madison was the brains and the energy that put our Constitution together, as well as our Bill of Rights.

The brilliance of the vision that was Madison's was carved out in lonely solitude at his family home at the foot of the Blue Ridge Mountains. He surrounded himself with history books. Thomas Jefferson kept sending them to his dear friend and kindred spirit.

For months on end Madison read and studied history, asking the question: "Why do nations fail?" And, here in this lonely intellectual and spiritual odyssey, the answer came to him that would change the world — weakness at the center. If power stayed in the hands of the states, we were sure to fail. The states would all exist as one United States.

Our first six presidents must be crying in their graves today. Our society is saturated with the lethal disease that they fought so hard against. I speak of the obscene wedding today between many politicians and orthodox Christianity.

We have a president who declared a recent year to be the "Year of the Bible," a president who speaks to national meetings of religious broadcasters and evangelicals.

These acts would be repugnant to our founders, whether Republican or Democrat. By stark contrast, our first six presidents refused all invitations for church membership. The Constitutional Convention would not even allow a prayer to open the meeting, they so wanted to keep religion out of it. There is no reference to God or Jesus in the Constitution of this country.

James Madison should be at the very front of our celebrations this year. He was the father of the Constitution and the Bill of Rights, both unique in the history of civilization.

Thomas Paine

It was Theodore Roosevelt who called Thomas Paine "the filthy little atheist."

What that stupid statement accomplished was only to prove the ignorance of Roosevelt. Thomas Paine, one of our giant founders, was not in any sense an atheist. He did have a total contempt for the *Bible*, the church and the clergy, as did our major Founding Fathers. But having a contempt for the *Bible* and the clergy does not, in any sense, make one an atheist.

Thomas Paine was a devout deist, who said and wrote time and time again "I believe in one God . . . ."

He also wrote "I would not dare to so dishonor my Creator God by attaching His name to that book (the *Bible*). Men and books lie. Only nature does not lie."

He explained what he meant in these words: "The character of Moses is the most horrid tale that can be imagined. Moses was a wretch that committed the most horrible atrocities that can be found in the literature of any nation. 'For Moses said unto them (according to the *Bible*) kill every male among the little ones, and kill every woman that hath known a man by lying with him, but all the women that have not known a man by lying with him, keep alive for yourselves.'

"Among the most detestable villains in history, you could not find one worse than Moses. Here is an order, attributed to 'God' to butcher the boys, to massacre the mothers and to debauch and rape the daughters. I would not dare so dishonor my Creator's name by (attaching) it to this filthy book."

And again, Paine wrote: "It is the duty of every true Deist to vindicate the moral justice of God against the evils of the *Bible*."

And again: "Accustom a people to believe that priests and clergy can forgive sins . . . and you will have sins in abundance."

And again: "The Christian church has set up a religion of pomp and revenue in pretended imitation of a person (Jesus) who lived a life of poverty."

We are celebrating the 200th anniversary of our Constitution this year, and it is especially fitting that we celebrate the life and the 250th birthday of Thomas Paine, who first gave us this group of words: "The United States of America."

George Washington read Paine's words to his troops to keep their morale high and their passions aflame. Abraham Lincoln said that he, daily, read the writings of Thomas Paine and Thomas Jefferson.

Thomas Edison paid this tribute to Paine: "When we consider Paine's planning of this great American republic, he may be justly considered the founder." James Madison wrote these words: "Paine's *The*

Rights of Man is the clearest exposition written of the principles on which the United States is founded."

It was Thomas Paine who gave us one of the most classic lines in all of literature, in words that should be over every church door, every school door, every state capitol, every government office and every judicial chamber: "Infidelity does not consist in believing or in disbelieving anything; but infidelity consists in professing to believe what a *person does not believe*. It is impossible to calculate the moral damage that mental lying has produced in society."

Andrew Jackson gives us our final word: "Thomas Paine has erected a monument in the hearts of all lovers of liberty. His *The Rights of Man* will be more enduring than all the piles of marble and granite that man can erect."

Paine did erect one of the great monuments of civilization. He called it . . . the United States of America.

"Thomas Paine may justly be considered the founder of the great American Republic."

— Thomas Edison

"Thomas Paine's The Rights of Man *is the clearest written exposition of the principles on which the United States is founded."*

— James Madison

John Adams

There was something mystical about the relationship between John Adams and Thomas Jefferson. On July 4, 1826, America celebrated the 50th anniversary of Independence. John Adams died on that day, saying "Jefferson lives," but on that same day, before sunset, Thomas Jefferson died.

It is a golden privilege to sit in your study in 1988 and, through the written word, listen to these two giants. To read the Jefferson-Adams letters and listen to them exchange ideas on practically every subject known to our species, is an inspirational and educational experience

Adams was a humanist who went no further in his theology than "in the beginning, God." He did not believe in the divinity of Jesus. He did not believe in the trinity or any of the other Christian doctrines, and the *Bible* was just another book to him. In fact, as with the others, he found Christian doctrine repugnant.

He had a contempt for the clergy and he looked upon the church as one of the great tyrannies that bound human minds and spirits. Naturally the clergy attacked him. John Adams responded to them in these words: "This is my religion, only this, my adoration for the creator of this magnificent universe, and delight, joy, triumph and exultation in my own existence. Even though I am only an atom, a molecule in the universe, that is all of my religion. So go ahead and snarl, bite and howl, all of you Christian Calvinistic Divines, and all of you who say that I am no Christian. Well, I say to you that you are no Christian . . . so there, the account is balanced."

Regarding the doctrine of the trinity, which all of our founders found absurd, Adams wrote these words to his friend Jefferson:

"Tom, had you and I been forty days with Moses, and even if the great God had tried to tell us that three was one, and one equals three, you and I would never have believed it, for you and I could never fall victim to the lie that 2 and 2 equals 5, for we know the contrary."

Adams signed the Treaty of Tripoli, with its article 11, which began "The Government of the United States is not in any sense founded on the Christian religion."

Adams was convinced that none of the Christian creeds and doctrines were in the *Bible*. They were all man-made to give the church and the clergy power. And so he wrote: "Where do we find a precept in the *Bible* for Creeds, Confessions, Doctrines and Oaths, and whole carloads of other trumpery that we find religion encumbered with in these days?"

And Adams continues: "The doctrine of the divinity of Jesus has made a convenient cover for absurdity."

One event in his life had a lasting effect upon him. In his own town, the minister of the First Congregational Church was recognized as the most scholarly minister in the town's history. But officers and members of the church did not like the scholarship that was being brought to them, and so they started a vicious campaign against this minister with the most slanderous character assassination.

They spread their poison throughout the area. It spread, in Adams' words, "by people, drunk on hate, a far more despicable intoxication than one who is intoxicated by only a beverage." Adams never again had any use for the church.

Episcopalian minister Bird Wilson, in a sermon of October 1831, summed up the religion of our founders in these words: "Among all of our Presidents, from Washington downward, not one was a professor of religion (Christianity), at least not of more than Unitarianism."

"The priesthood have, in all nations, monopolized learning, and ever since the Reformation where or when has existed a Protestant or dissenting sect who would tolerate a FREE INQUIRY or free thought. The most un-gentlemanly insolence, the most yahooish brutality, is patiently endured, countenanced, propagated, and applauded. But touch solemn truth in colli-sion with a dogma of a sect, though capable of the clearest proof, and you will soon find that you have disturbed a nest, and the hornets will swarm about your eyes and hands, and fly into your face and eyes."

— John Adams

"A man more perfectly honest never issued from the hands of his Crea-tor."

— Thomas Jefferson speaking of John Adams

George Washington

Historians have noted that more myths have been created about George Washington than any of the other founders. It was an Anglican minister, Mason Weems, who invented the famous cherry tree story, as well as many others about Washington's 'religion.' The following quotes from Washington will give you some flavor of his religious thought.

"Being no bigot myself, I am disposed to indulge the teachers of Christianity and the church."

When looking for servants, he wrote that he would be happy to have "Mohammedans, Jews, Christians or atheists." Episcopalian minister Bird Wilson, in a sermon delivered in 1831, stated that "Washington is no more than a Unitarian, if anything."

The minister, James Abercrombie, criticized Washington from the pulpit for not kneeling and not taking communion. Washington did not again attend any church services. Wrote Washington: "Religious controversies are always productive of more irreconcilable hatreds than those which spring from any other cause." Historians write that the famous picture of Washington kneeling in prayer at Valley Forge is nothing more than the wild imagination of the artist. Washington never kneeled to pray, not even in church.

I recently read the finest definition of 'evil' that I have ever come across: "Evil . . . is *militant ignorance.*" I thought of it when I read the utter stupidity of a Jerry Falwell statement: "The idea that church and state should be separated was invented by the devil to keep us Christians from running this country."

All of the founders were adamant in *demanding* an absolute separation of church and state. The most important expression of this principle is in the Treaty of Tripoli, under Washington. Article Eleven begins: "As the government of the United States is NOT IN ANY SENSE founded on the Christian religion . . . " This treaty was ratified by the senate in 1797 without a SINGLE OBJECTION. And so, let me make this very clear, underlined, in five colors, with a spotlight bathing it in light: The United States of America, according to the founders, was not in any sense founded upon the Christian religion, and this fact is in the Constitution that we are now celebrating. Article 6 of the U.S. Constitution made this treaty doubly binding by saying this: "All treaties made, or which shall be made, under the authority of the United States shall be bound thereby, anything in the laws of any state to the contrary notwithstanding." Thus was article eleven of the Treaty of Tripoli made valid for the United States. It should today be treasured as the supreme document for the American doctrine of the *absolute* separation of church and state.

The next time that you read, or hear, statements by the political and Christian 'right' that totally pervert and prostitute the intent and the beliefs of our founding fathers, you might remember that perfect definition of evil: 'militant ignorance.' Or maybe that great genius, Goethe, said it better: "Nothing is more terrifying than . . . ignorance in action."

"Washington refused to kneel for prayer, and refused to take communion when he attended the Episcopal Church."

— Martha Washington

More about George Washington

When I started this series on the religion of our Founding Fathers, I gave two reasons why I thought it would be educational and interesting. One: very few Americans know anything about the subject. Two: the fact that the Christian 'right' (fundamentalists), with the political 'right,' are always misrepresenting and adulterating our Founders' religious beliefs. Now, I never dreamed that I would have such a marvelous opportunity to illustrate that second reason, but a perfect example has fallen into my lap on a silver platter. My recent column on George Washington brought out the fact that Washington was one of our least religious Presidents, or as Episcopalian minister Bird Wilson, in 1831, said in a sermon "Washington was no more than a Unitarian, if anything."

Then, lo and behold, on Sunday, a letter to the editor appeared in our newspaper written by an "associate pastor of the Glad Tidings Church in Boise." In that letter, after calling my columns 'unscholarly,' and worse, he then wrote that he was going to quote words from "Washington's *own book*, in his *own hand*," a book, and words, that were apparently 'unknown to me' he wrote. He was right. His quote was 'unknown to me.' I have since made the enlightening discovery that the book and quote are also totally 'unknown' to the Reference and Research Division of the Library of Congress in Washington, D.C., as well as the Boise Public Library and the Boise State University library. In his letter to the editor, the pastor wrote: "A quotation from George Washington's OWN BOOK, written in his OWN HAND, titled *Daily Sacrifice* will put things back in perspective," and then included in the quote, in 'Washington's own hand' is this 100% fundamentalist language: "Wash away my sins in the immaculate Blood of the Lamb . . . and daily frame me more and more into the likeness of Thy Son Jesus Christ." Well now, any sophomoric student of Washington and his religion would know, without even a second glance, that the book and the quote are phony. Washington would have found such fundamentalist language totally repugnant. The Library of Congress confirmed that no such book ever existed or that Washington could have written such words.

As an additional reference I called the Director of Religious Studies, who is also a Professor of Philosophy at the University of Idaho. He is one of the leading scholars in the northwest on the religion of our Founders. When I read the quote to him on the phone, he started laughing and responded with "what a monstrous fraud." In his book *George Washington and Religion*, Professor Paul Boller of the University of Massachusetts writes: "In all of Washington's voluminous writing, only ONCE does he even speak of Jesus, and this single incident was in a speech to the Delaware Indians, and penned in by an aide." The reference had nothing to do with Washington's theology or beliefs about Jesus.

As a closing thought: The pastor from Boise told me on the telephone that he 'had read' that the book he quoted from, George Washington's "own book written in his own hand," could be found in the Yale University Divinity School library. Naturally, I called the head Reference Librarian of the Yale Divinity School. He too laughed, saying that, quote: "no such book existed" and that "Washington would never have used such fundamentalist language."

Washington was deist, humanist and, as many scholars have noted, was probably the least religious of any of our first six Presidents.

Abraham Lincoln

Even though Abraham Lincoln was not one of our Founding Fathers, literally, he was such a giant in American history that I close my series on their religious orientation with this man whose memorial stands with Jefferson's in Washington, D.C.

Lincoln has been portrayed in more books and articles, and in more languages in more countries than any other American. He almost idolized Thomas Paine and Thomas Jefferson and studied their writings in exhaustive detail.

Lincoln refused to be baptized or to join any Christian church. His wife said: "My husband is not a Christian . . . but he is a religious man I think."

Lincoln wrote these words: "I have never united myself to any church, because I could not give assent to the long, complicated statements of Christian doctrine and dogma which characterize their articles of belief. When any church will inscribe over its alter . . . as the sole qualification for membership, only the Great Commandment to love God and neighbour, that church will I join."

Following the death of Lincoln, the most eloquent eulogies came from the Jewish community. Rabbi Nathan Krass, in Buffalo, New York, used these words: "It is said that Mr. Lincoln was no churchman . . . and we know that is true. Well, what of it? The great religious giants of history were not churchmen. The prophets were not churchmen. Jesus was no churchman, and would not be so even today. Yet in their hearts was the spirit of God that transcends the church."

By contrast, the Rev. Dr. Gurley, Presbyterian minister of Washington, D.C., in a sermon he called "The Voice of the Rod" told his congregation that it would always be a tragedy to "good Christians everywhere, and God, that Lincoln fell in a theater." He continued: "Multitudes of Christians would have preferred that he be killed anywhere but in a theater, the last place that any good Christian should be, and certainly the last place that any good Christian should die."

Lincoln loved to tell stories and jokes that were in the manner of Mark Twain. His favorite jokes were what he called his preacher stories. Needless to say, the clergy of that day did not find them amusing, nor would many of them today. A number of years ago, I discovered a marvelous little book called "Lincoln's Preacher Stories."

Many are so ribald, of course, that I cannot print them.

But a few of his favorites: "A young intelligent Unitarian minister came to Springfield, Illinois. He was becoming so popular that the other orthodox ministers in town decided to preach against him. They flipped a coin to see who would preach the first sermon against this Unitarian minister. It fell to the Methodist minister, who started out by telling his congregation how happy they should all be in their orthodox church and then he started getting really warmed up — and shouted to people . . . , 'And now . . . AND NOW . . . there comes into town this Unitarian kid . . . preaching a doctrine that all men and women are going to be saved . . . that all men and women are going with us to heaven . . . brethren . . . oh brethren . . . let us hope for better things.'"

A delegation of clergy once called on Lincoln to explain Christian doctrine to him. Lincoln became more and more exasperated, and finally broke in and said "Reverend, if you call a sheep's tail a leg, how many legs will the sheep have?"

Visibly taken back, the Reverend spokesman said, "Why five, of course." "No sir," said Lincoln, "You are wrong reverend . . . because calling a sheep's tail a leg don't make it so." Thus ended the interview with the clergy.

As to Lincoln's religion, his private secretary said it best: "He believed in the practice of justice and mercy . . . that was his religion, and the world can utter no other verdict than this."

Wedding of Religion and Politics

As a religion columnist, I feel perfectly free, even obligated, to make observations about the horrendous wedding of religion and politics by the current administration.

President Reagan's address before the religious broadcasters was one of the most frightening political events that I have witnessed, in this country, in my lifetime. His alliance with a fundamentalist preacher who could make the following statement is morally repugnant.

"I hope and pray for the day when we won't have any more public schools. The churches will have taken them all over again and Christians will be running them," Jerry Falwell proclaimed recently in one of his sermons.

Fanaticism is too weak a word here; perhaps religious insanity is more near the truth. Last summer Falwell played a major role in shaping the most extreme right-wing Republican platform in years. He visits the White House often and prays over Republican gatherings. To cheering Republicans in Dallas, Falwell declared that Reagan and Bush were "God's chosen instruments."

Any number of Falwell's colleagues attend Reagan's religious meetings, such as the Rev. James Robison, who once declared that "non-Christians cannot understand spiritual things," and the Rev. Pat Robertson who made the idiotic remark that "our form of government comes directly out of the *Bible*."

Martin Marty, professor of church history at the University of Chicago, wrote that "people think they are hearing the old-time religion from Falwell, but it is not that at all. It is only 20th century White House politics."

I don't have space to critique it here, but President Reagan's August 23 prayer breakfast address, on religion in America, could well have been one of the most confused, misinformed, ignorant and misleading addresses in the entire history of the American presidency.

Any student of history will compare this pathetic attempt to pervert the history of church and state in America with the statesman-like leadership of our founding fathers on this subject. Thomas Jefferson, in a letter to Samuel Miller, January 23, 1808, wrote: "Certainly, no power to prescribe ANY religious exercise, or to assume ANY authority in religious discipline, has been delegated to the general government. Prayer is a religious exercise. The government has not been invested with the power of effecting ANY uniformity of time or matter regarding religious exercises. CIVIL POWERS ALONE have been given to the President of the United States."

Or, listen to his magnificent statement of religious morality and ethics written to Dr. Benjamin Rush, April 21, 1803: "I am adverse to the communication of my personal religious tenets to the public, because it would seduce public opinion to erect itself into that inquisition over the rights of conscience, which the LAWS HAVE SO JUSTLY PROSCRIBED."

Religion, with our founding fathers, had to be protected against the government itself acting in the name of religion.

Oh, for men or women of that intelligence, that character, that quality again.

The time is short.

The hour is late.

The Hypocrisy of Politicians on Religion

All of this talk coming from the president of the United States, and others, about the wedding of religion and politics is scaring me to death.

I care not if it is a Republican or Democratic president. I remember how easy it was for Germany to slide into the Nazi mentality in the name of "God and country." A "God-chosen master race" was the dream of Germany. We are all entitled to stupid statements from time to time, but for our president to be continually mouthing religious absurdities is embarrassing to any intelligent 6th grader. I only have space enough to mention two:

1. He stated that "morality's foundation is religion." Apparently he has never been exposed to the "religious morality" of the Crusades, the Inquisition, the burning of Salem witches, the religious bloodbath of today's Ireland, the bombings of Beirut by religious terrorists, the Ku Klux Klan reading from the *Bible* while torturing blacks, Iran and Iraq, and where would it end?

By contrast many agnostics, atheists and others who have rejected all forms of organized and institutional religion have lived lives of magnificent morality. To equate morality and religion is to reach the heights of absurdity.

2. His statement that "it's time to say 'No' to those who want to keep God out of our public school classrooms." Does God really need Ronald Reagan, or any of us, to look out after Him? Assuming protection for God reaches heights of idiocy. God hardly needs the help of politicians to keep Him alive.

I have often wondered why so many are so nervous about God, on this little speck called Earth, only a grain of sand on the cosmic beach. We must be continually reminded that "In God We Trust" or we might relax and trust someone or something else. Many seem to think that God needs all the help we can give Him and that unless we continually brace Him up He might fall apart. And if we were to doubt or question, God might just dissolve. In my more quiet moments, I would think that if God needs all this much protection He cannot be much of a God.

I would suggest that God needs no protectors. If God is in as bad a shape as that, that He needs Reagan and Falwell for protection, then folks, the jig is up and there is no use pretending any longer.

I know of few issues more dangerous to this nation than this Reagan-Falwell type wedding of religion and politics. The Queen of England is the "defender of the faith." The president of the United States is the defender of the Constitution, the defender of ALL faiths: Buddhist,

Taoist, Jewish, Hindu, Christian, agnostic, atheist, Druid or what have you.

John O'Connor, the new Roman Catholic Bishop of New York, said that "Reagan is using religion as a tool." To surround a political campaign with religious trappings is a sham, a sham in religion's name. True, deep and profound religion is a very personal thing and can never, never be orchestrated by a federal government or anyone else.

We are being assaulted with religious sham. It is a sacrilege, but far worse, the ultimate in religious hypocrisy.

A Greek oracle says it all: "Summoned or not summoned, God is here."

"Honor is a word that could, if believed in by enough people, completely destroy totalitarianism as it expresses itself in other countries and in our own. For it gives dignity and value to a man's personal and public relationships; it makes means as important as ends; it confers quality on experience.

"You can gauge how much real quality there is in a country by the value its people put on their individual honor."

— The Journey,
Lilian Smith

24

Pat Robertson and Ignorance

While eating breakfast several weeks ago in Bend, Oregon, I was reading an interview in the morning newspaper with multimillionaire television fundamentalist evangelist Pat Robertson. It was religion, politics, power and *money* . . . It was all I could do to get through my breakfast, while gagging at every paragraph.

He first informed me that he wanted to "return this nation to 'biblical' morality." That brought to my mind a cartoon that was recently printed in the *Kansas City Times,* drawn by their own political cartoonist. The entire picture was just of the *Bible,* and at the top were these words: "For those of you who like to ban books, here's one with immorality, lust, sex, racism, homosexuality, prostitution, rape, violence, incest and murder."

Underneath those words was the large drawing of the *Bible.* Robertson never did say which one of those 'moralities' he wants to return us to.

Pat Robertson for president. Can you believe it? Our brilliant founding fathers, Thomas Jefferson, James Madison, John Adams, Benjamin Franklin and the rest must be in total shock and disbelief. They despised fundamentalism and biblical fundamentalist preachers and said so in many of their writings and letters that are now public.

Next, Pat Robertson informed me that he has "medical verification" that he has healed "tens of thousands" of people. That's what he said folks, "tens of thousands." Jesus must be consumed with jealousy and green with envy. He never healed in his lifetime tens of thousands, but only a few. And the disciples of Jesus tried to heal, but they were not able, as the gospels tell us.

Pat Robertson should let them in on his secret. Those who lived with Jesus could not do what Pat says he is doing.

I haven't come to the really good parts yet. He went on to say, "The enemies of the U.S. are enemies of the Lord." Get that? Don't miss it. The Lord and the United States are buddies.

The Lord is a right-wing fundamentalist republican, with a button-down collar. The stupidity of these kinds of statements preclude any intelligent response. But now, for his closing statement . . . Are you ready for this? "We religious broadcasters are a symbol, a symbol for spiritual renewal." There would be far more truth in the statement that "we religious broadcasters are a symbol for superstition, ignorance, fear and a symbol for power, politics and money."

Upon returning to my hotel room, I told my wife that I hoped lunch went better . . . like outside in some clean, fresh air, where the spiritual can truly be experienced . . . with God's pure revelation.

HUMANISM

Proud to be a Humanist

H. L. Mencken, the renowned syndicated columnist for the *Baltimore Sun,* once wrote that he had no need ever to attend a circus.

Why?

Because he lived in a society that was a circus, with clowns everywhere. Mark Twain made similar observations.

I always remember Mencken's words when I read the rantings and ravings of those aiming their tirades at some mirage they call "secular humanism."

There was a wonderful cartoon recently in the *Washington Post.* The picture is of a man and his wife dressed in very puritan, "do-good" clothing. She is holding a book called *The Book Hit List.* He's reading from a newspaper.

The man says: "Holy Guacamole! Here's a story about a school system that doesn't pervert children's minds with philosophy, literature, social studies, the arts, history and the rest of that secular humanism bunk!"

The woman responds: "Halleluia! Where is it?"

The man answers: "Russia."

How individual members of the fanatical right define "secular humanism" depends on where they are on a scale of 1 to 10 of brain constipation.

An example: In a pamphlet entitled "Is Humanism Molesting Your Child?" a Texas parents' group described "secular humanism" in these words: "A belief in the distribution of wealth . . . control of the environment, control of energy and its limitation . . . the removal of the free enterprise system . . . working for disarmament . . . and the creation of world government."

For some, attacking "secular humanism" means taking great literature out of our schools. That's called book burning, which they did in Nazi Germany. It means not exposing our young people to what a small group of parents have decided is "obscene."

By their own standards and definitions, they will have to ban the *Bible* from home and school libraries, for the *Bible* is full of every obscenity known to the human race — rape, gang rape, sodomy, adultery, genocide, incest, and all in lurid detail.

What extremists do to magnificent words and ideas is frightening. Humanism, for example, is one of the most beautiful words in our language. A vast majority of everything that an enlightened citizenry cherishes is due to "humanism." My *Webster's New Collegiate Dictionary* defines humanism as "a devotion to the humanities . . . literary culture . . . the revival of the classics . . . a philosophy that asserts the dignity and worth of human beings."

And from the Columbia University Encyclopedia Britannica: "Humanism . . . the distinctive characteristic of the Renaissance . . . an emphasis on classical studies . . . a conscious return to classical ideas. Contemporary meanings of the word emphasize lasting human values with a cultivation of the classics."

We were rescued from ignorance and the Dark Ages by the Renaissance and the humanists. Scholars were once again recognized as the cream of society and politics. The humanists became advisers and counselors to senators, dukes and popes.

As the historian Will Durant put it in his volume, *Renaissance*: "They (the humanists) transformed the ideal of a gentleman from a man with a ready sword and clanking spurs into that of the fully developed individual attaining to wisdom and worth by absorbing the cultural heritage of the race. The prestige of their learning, combined with their eloquence, conquered Europe. Country after country was inoculated with the new culture, and passed from medievalism to modernity. It was the humanist who liberated man from dogma, taught him to love life rather than brood about death, and made the European mind free."

How proud I am to be associated with humanists, humanitarians, the humanities and all that it means to be truly human in the most noble sense — as one devoted to the classics and emphasizing lasting human values.

Humankind is still our main business. And humankind is what the humanities and humanists are all about.

The Need for Humanists

Perhaps the most ludicrous and asinine charge made by those ranting against "humanists" is that they are "godless." A list of brilliant humanists, who were also deeply religious and spiritual persons in the most profound sense, would be endless: Plato, Aristotle, Erasmus, Montaigne, Sir Thomas More, Paracelsus, and one of the greatest thinkers of the 15th century, Nicolaus Cusanus, Sir Francis Bacon, Goethe, Albert Schweitzer and practically all of our major founding fathers, from Thomas Jefferson to Abraham Lincoln.

One of the most beautiful books in my library is entitled *Humanist Meditations* by the Hebrew scholar Emil Weitzner. His entire book creates an atmosphere of holiness. In his introduction he writes of "that mystery which keeps our biological and moral existence together, that impenetrable darkness in which God, the mystery dwells. It is a paradox that as knowledge increases, the mystery deepens. For all that we are, for all that we know, for life unfolding in its wonder and beauty, its promise and its hope, let us in the sight of the mystery give thanks."

The motivation of the humanistic movement in the 14th century was to produce a fully cultivated human being. Educational programs were upgraded and refined. The inner needs of the religious life combined with a classical education became the ideal.

Children studied the Latin classics; they read history, ethics, poetry and drama; they learned to compose in both Latin and Greek. Music and singing were required. The sciences were mandatory: geometry, astronomy and natural history. With this curriculum, designed for mental development, were rigorous courses in physical education. Training in riding and swimming and other outdoor activities was compulsory.

Along with these subjects was one overall, pervasive, theme. It was the cultivation of manners that one needed to become a fully civilized human being. Would to God that we could revive this humanistic concept, of what it means to be a fully developed person, in today's educational programs.

Erasmus (1466-1536) was the greatest classical scholar of his day. Carl Jung thought Erasmus one of the brightest lights of civilization.

Erasmus spent his adult life attempting to clean out the superstitions of the religion of his day and reforming the corrupt church. With his sharpest needles he continually punctured the ignorance of the clergy and he poured scorn on what he called "the vulgar and superstitious versions of Christianity being taught."

Erasmus and the other humanists of this period revealed and exposed the 16th century church as a monstrous and sick aberration. Their brilliance and eloquence, combined with vast scholarship, spread far and wide and was a tremendous impetus for religious enlightenment.

Our Founding Fathers, as humanists with a profound sense of the mystery, carried on within this tradition and in like manner attacked, in scathing words, the superstitions, doctrines and bigotry of the Christian clergy and church in their own day, hoping to let in some much needed fresh air.

Humanists — schooled in the humanities and other liberal arts — combining the needs of the spiritual life with a classical education — whether theist, deist, Christian, Buddhist, Taoist or Hebrew — could very well be the bright hope of this nation.

Jesus Was a Great Humanist

The fact that Jesus was one of civilization's greatest humanists must be like a bur under the saddle blanket for those who spend mindless hours blabbing about the "evils" of humanism.

In religious humanism, people are the first and primary consideration. People are more important than authoritarian, dogmatic, brittle, religious laws, creeds, rules, theologies, beliefs and man-made doctrines. In a very blunt and direct attack on such absurdities, Jesus placed humans front and foremost.

Nothing so infuriated him as to see religious doctrine become more important than people. It was against the religious law to feed or heal a person on the Sabbath. With scathing words, Jesus let them know that "the sabbath was made for people . . . people were NOT made for the sabbath." (Mark 2:27)

Religious laws and institutions are not sacred. Creeds are not sacred. Theological dogma is not sacred. Man-made doctrines are not sacred. Jesus attacked authoritarian religion at every turn, replacing it with a humanitarian, humanistic religion.

Jesus' insistence that "the kingdom of God is within you," as well as many other biblical passages, is a clear expression of a non-authoritarian position.

The spirit behind his parables and teachings is totally humanistic with a blinding emphasis on the importance of human beings, their needs, their potential, their divinity — pointing the way toward the full development of the human potential for excellence, love and brotherhood.

The vast majority of the evils inflicted upon humankind today are the product of dogmatic, religious authoritarianism — not humanism.

If you can bear to read the history of the Christian Church after it departed from humanism, I encourage you to do so. The beauty, goodness and justice of humanism will become obvious when placed alongside the hundreds of thousands of people tortured and killed by the authoritarian church.

Look at Islamic fundamentalists, dogmatic Protestants and Catholics killing each other off in Ireland, the nightmare of Beirut and the surrounding area, the recent grotesque performance of a fundamentalist minister leading his congregation in prayer for the death of U.S. Supreme Court Justice William Brennan.

The followers and propagators of dogmatic, authoritarian religion all have the same mentality, whether "Christian," Communist or Nazi, as Eric Hoffer wrote in his classic *The True Believer*. They live with the fantasy that only they possess the truth.

From my Columbia University Encyclopedia: "Humanism . . . a way of life, and a philosophy that asserts the dignity and worth of human beings and their capacity for self-realization and an emphasis on lasting human values."

"Teachers of religion must have the stature to give up the archaic doctrine of a personal God, that is, give up the source of fear which has only placed vast power in the hands of the clergy and priests. Such a doctrine is not only unworthy, but fatal, and has done incalculable harm to human spiritual progress."

— Albert Einstein,
Nobel Prize winner in PHYSICS

THE CHURCH, THE BIBLE AND JESUS

What Do You Mean by God?

Alfred North Whitehead wrote: "The most important single question facing modern human beings is this: 'What do you mean by God?'"

The answer contains perhaps the most profound difference between Zen/Taoism and orthodox Christianity. The word "God" means nothing in itself. It's only a symbol for a cosmic force, a metaphysical abstraction, a divine principle, a he, she or it, a supermyth, a mother hen.

A number of years ago a major Protestant denomination took a poll among grade school children and adults who had been active in church school. They were asked: "How do you think of God?"

Are you ready for this? The adults gave exactly the same answers as the grade school children, but with a different choice of words. God turned out to be either a cosmic bellhop, just waiting for you to ring, via prayer. Or else he was seen as a celestial hitman who took John in an early death — for "it was God's will you know." Sometimes God was a divine window peeker, constantly watching to make sure you're being good — the ultimate voyeur.

It's impossible to understand how so many could still, in 1988, be so buried in this archaic and primitive anthropomorphism. You remember the definition of anthropomorphism. Anytime you attribute human emotions or conduct to anything non-human, you are creating an anthropomorphism. You say, for example, "listen to the birds, how joyful they are." You don't really know whether the birds are joyful. You are joyful and so transfer a human emotion to the birds.

When it comes to God, orthodox Christianity still is buried in that debris. The *Bible* is loaded with anthropomorphisms. We take every human emotion and then transfer it to something non-human, God.

We say God "loves," God "forgives, judges," is "jealous," is "angry," and so on. All we are doing is transferring a human emotion to some supernatural "it" that lives just on the other side of Mars. We still think of a God "out there," as though it is God and us, God and the creation — as though God is something apart from everything else.

A Zen master explained how childish this view is considered in Zen thought: "God against man . . . man against God; God against nature, nature against God; man against nature . . . nature against man . . . a very, very funny religion."

Thousands and thousands of ministers tell people all about God. They talk about what this God wants, expects, likes, dislikes, loves and hates. They talk about what movies and books he approves of, and on and on, with one absurdity piled on top of another.

Those same ministers cannot even explain how a light bulb works. Yet, without a moment's blush or embarrassment, they will tell people all about the mystery behind a million galaxies, and what that same mystery expects you to do today.

When Mircea Eliade was chairman of the Department of Religion at the University of Chicago, he wrote: "all talk as to the nature of God, in a universe composed of millions of galaxies, including probably a million inhabited planets, is naive and childish beyond description."

This issue highlights the most profound difference between Zen / Taoism and orthodox Christianity.

"God . . . someone from another planet more developed than ours."

— one of my students

"God . . . a good psychiatrist."

— another of my students

"God . . . someone I should be like."

— Ibid

"God . . . a no fault counselor."

— Ibid

"God . . . he is my Dad."

— Ibid

"God . . . I discuss things with him . . . and he discusses things with me."

— Ibid

"Bible" Christians

I don't know of any phrase that is more meaningless and nonsensical than "a *Bible* Christian." You constantly hear it or else read it in letters to the editor.

To illustrate this point, I used to invite representatives from ten different "Christian" groups to speak to my university class about their beliefs.

Usually I would start with a Christian Science practitioner (who was always the best prepared). Next would be the Jehovah Witnesses (who always came in threes). Then: Seventh Day Adventists, Mormons, Pentecostals, a Roman Catholic priest, a Unity minister, Greek Orthodox, a Unitarian minister, Missouri Synod Lutheran and Methodist and/or Presbyterian. They all quoted from the *Bible* to affirm and justify their positions. The students soon realized they were listening to ten totally different religions, all calling themselves "Christian" and all reading from the same book, to prove their beliefs.

No other religion studied by historians has been — or is — so completely fragmented and splintered as the one we call "Christianity." Protestantism alone has disintegrated into more than 400 different denominations, all quoting from the *Bible* to "prove" or validate their beliefs. Can you see why the phrase *"Bible* Christian" is nonsensical?

All anyone can say, with any degree of honesty, is that "I am a Seventh Day Adventist, Protestant person, who finds what I want in a book called the *Bible,* and I like to think that it makes me a 'Christian'". And that statement would be made by others in more than 400 different and splintered Protestant denominations, and by the Greek Orthodox and Roman Catholics as well.

There is also the pathetic spectacle of many of these denominations telling other "Christian" groups — such as the Mormons, Unitarians, Christian Scientists and the members of Unity — that they aren't really "Christians" at all, although they all are using the same *Bible.* Added to this is the practice of some Protestant denominations — notably the Missouri Synod Lutherans — who refuse to allow any of the other 399 "Christian" groups even to enter their church and share The Lord's Supper service with them. Protestants and Roman Catholics are murdering each other off just as fast as they can find bombs and bullets in Ireland's blood bath, and all are reading from the *Bible* to justify their violence.

How well did Thomas Jefferson prophesy that "Christian creeds, doctrines, formulas and dogmas, the clergies' own fatal inventions, will someday be the ruin of the Christian church and will make of Christendom a slaughterhouse, dividing it into castes, with intolerable hatred, one for the other."

We do not have to go to Ireland to observe the slaughter in the name of the *Bible* and "Christianity." We can stay right in our own backyard. There is perhaps no other fight in society that is any more vicious than church fights, even within one denomination, or one building — whether it is over the new organist, the minister, the new rug, or what have you. And every faction offers the lamentable spectacle of being helplessly caught in the chains of its own imagined and phantasmic righteousness, trapped in its own dead-end creedal canyon.

Christian "love" has invoked or participated in some of the greatest blood baths in the history of civilization, from the Crusades through the Inquisition to the Salem Witch Trials.

It is long past time for us so-called "Christians," regardless of denomination, to take a long, hard look at ourselves, the games we play and the masks we wear that are totally antithetical to the Man of Nazareth and all that he represented.

We will never be redeemed by any archaic system of theology, but only by the birth of a new consciousness with an accompanying spirituality. New spiritual forms and symbols must be born. Our species and our planet waits.

All of the "Christian" denominations have the choice to participate in the creation of a new consciousness for the race, or the alternative, to continue to be a detriment to such an enlightened consciousness through the divisive creeds and doctrines of manmade formulas.

As Carl Jung wrote of his Swiss Lutheran pastor father: "my father's *Bible* stood as a great wall between him and the Living God."

May all of the churches calling themselves Christian move with creativity, courage and risk taking into the formation of a new consciousness for this new and perilous age.

And it just might happen that "swords will be beaten into plowshares, and spears into pruning hooks" over our entire beloved planet Earth. It begins with you, with me. Surely, that is a worthy prayer.

Worship of the Bible . . .
a Malignant Disease

For a great many the *Bible* itself has become an object of worship, an idol. Perhaps the most malignant disease in the Christian church today, I believe, is biblical literalism: believing that every word is to be read as the divine, without error, word of God.

The Oxford Universal Dictionary defines Christian fundamentalism in these words: " . . . strict adherence to a literal inerrancy of the *Bible.*" Inerrancy means "without error."

The irony of all this is that anyone with exposure to church history knows that a great many of our more eminent church fathers, theologians and biblical scholars have either thrown out, or ignored, various sections of the *Bible* as not being authentic or worthy of canonization.

Martin Luther, the father of our Protestant Reformation, called the book of Esther a ringing tale of sex and slaughter. His loathing of the Jews was an extension of his view of the Old Testament, which he did not regard as divine. He called the Book of James in the New Testament a "book of straw," and he would have nothing to do with the Book of Revelation, viewing it as beyond human reason or comprehension.

I could continue through church history with similar illustrations. The stupidities of biblical literalism defy the imagination. Example: If I wrote a column stating that we, as human beings, are nothing but animals, like all other animals, and nothing more, I would be excoriated as a "secular humanist," a blasphemer, an atheist and one who did not believe in the *Bible.*

And yet God's "without error" word tells me just that. In Chapter 3 of the Book of Ecclesiastes, God tells us: " . . . the sons of men may see that they are but as beasts. For the fate of the sons of men and the fate of beasts is the same: as one dies, so dies the other. They all have the same breath, and man has no advantage over the beasts; all go to one place; all are from the dust and all turn to dust again."

I believe the fundamentalist view of the *Bible* is not only infantile, but worse, it is religious blasphemy that condones ignorance and superstition and violates the sacred soul of human beings. Biblical verses are tortured out of context to support fundamentalist doctrines.

An example, recounted to me recently, was of a *Bible* school teacher telling a young child that "she killed Jesus and because of her sins the Son of God had to die."

What evil! What a dastardly think to do to a child. This type of biblical presentation is a nightmare, a hideous and horrible fantasy.

The brilliant founding fathers of this nation despised such clergy, and "despised" is their word, not mine. They despised those doctrines and everything they represented.

Thomas Jefferson referred to their *Bible* as a "dunghill." The columnist H. L. Mencken of the *Baltimore Evening Sun* wrote in 1928: "Millions of Americans, far from being free human beings, are the slaves of the ignorant, impudent and unconscionable clergy. They have dredged up theological ideas so preposterous that they would make an intelligent Zulu laugh. It has been made plain that this theology is not merely a harmless aberration, but rather the foundations of a way of life, bellicose, domineering, brutal and malignant."

Don't miss the most tragic irony, that a Jew named Jesus spoke, taught and reacted with anger, against all that "biblical," legalistic, fundamentalism represented in his own time with the literalistic Pharisees.

The untold misery that has been heaped upon the human race by biblical literalists is one of the great crimes of human history.

The Horror of Biblical 'Gods'

From time to time, as all writers do, I receive anonymous letters. In a number of such letters I have been asked: "Why don't you quote God, instead of men?"

That always reminds me of a great cartoon in the *New Yorker* magazine a number of years ago. A minister is standing, robed, in his pulpit with waving arms and he is saying "and now, reading from the *Bible*, God says . . . and I quote of course."

To deal with this question, I thought that a little multiple choice survey might help.

1. Which of the following "Gods" would they like me to quote? Yahweh; Elohim; Ahura Mazda; Ra; Osiris; Zeus; Jupiter; Dionysus; Demeter; Asklepios; Hermes; Aton; Odin; Thor; Varuna; Shang-ti; Amaterasu-Omikami . . . Oh well, that's enough — and we have not even touched on the goddesses.

2. If it's Biblical "gods" they're interested in, I am curious as to which one they would like quoted. Yahweh; Elohim; Hadad; El Shaddai; the Ba'alim; Anath; the anthropomorphic "God" who walked and talked in the garden; the "God" and his sons who came down from the mountaintop to sire children by earth women, *(Genesis)*; the jealous and vindictive "god"; the "god" of war; the "God" who was "spirit" (Jesus); the "God" who was "love", *(John)*. And that is only a few of the options.

3. I assume that those asking such a question still believe, even in 1988, that the *Bible* is the "infallible," "without error" "word" of God. So which of the following Biblical stories would they like me to write a column on for moral and spiritual edification?

The lovely, inspirational story of how Lot's two daughters gave him wine and then went to bed with him, and conceived by him. *(Genesis 19:30-38)* Today, we call it incest. Of course it could be called "holy debauchery," I guess.

Or, there is the rape of Tamar by her brother Amnon. "Do not force me" she pleaded, but he, "being stronger than she" just went right ahead. *(2 Samuel; 13:14)*

Or a little gang rape by God's "without error" word might uplift our readers. In the *Book of Judges*, Chapter 19, verse 25, we are inspired by the story of a gang of men who took a woman and "abused her all the night long until the morning." Then in verse 29, we are moved to new spiritual heights as they took a knife and carved her up into 12 pieces.

Let us consider genocide. That is where you wipe out an entire cultural group. Now, our "man of God," Moses did just that. In the *Book of Numbers* Chapter 31, Moses gives this command: "kill all of the men, and all of the male children, and kill all of the women who have had intercourse with a man, but *keep for yourselves the young women who are virgins.*"

And "God" "blessed" all of that carnage, rape, murder and genocide. Is that the "god" they wanted "quoted" from the "without error" "word"?

"Any system of religion that has anything in it that would shock the mind of a child, cannot be a true system," wrote Thomas Paine.

4. Which of the current, popular concepts of "God" would they like for me to write about? God as "divine windowpeeker," God as "cosmic bellhop," God as "celestial hitman"?

Is it not time that we said — with honesty and integrity — that the majority of the Biblical concepts of "God" are archaic and an insult to contemporary knowledge and spirituality?

People who cannot even explain a light bulb go around telling us all about "God" — the mystery that is behind *One Hundred Billion Major Galaxies.* They can't explain a radio, but "God" they know all about.

Other Great Religious Books

The Layman's Theological Library series of 12 volumes has been used by literally thousands of Protestant churches in America for adult study classes.

The volume *Understanding the Bible* was written by Dr. Fred Denbeaux, professor of Biblical Literature at Wellesley College, Massachusetts. His doctorate is from Union Theological Seminary in New York City. These words of his set my theme for this column: "The *Bible* is not the only religious book in the world, and a childish pride should not make us claim that it is even the most important religious book in the world. It cannot be made into a source for all wisdom, for it is not. The *Bible* is only one important religious book among other important religious books." And so it is.

There are magnificent sections of literature, prose, poetry and myth in the *Bible*. There are also brilliant insights into truth in all of the great religious literature of humankind. In Biblical literature sections of the book of *Ecclesiastes* are among my favorites: "All is vanity. What does man gain by all the toil at which he toils under the sun? A generation goes, and a generation comes, but the earth remains. The sun rises and the sun goes down, and hastens to the place where it rises. The wind blows to the south, and goes round to the north; round and round goes the wind, and on its circuits the wind returns. All streams run to the sea, but the sea is not full; to the place where the streams flow, there they flow again. What has been is what will be, and what has been done is what will be done; and there is nothing new under the sun. Is there a thing of which it is said, 'See, this is new?' It has been already, in the ages before us."

In the Rig-Veda, the core of Hindu scripture, I find the most magnificent creative poetry ever written in the Hymn of Creation: "Let us bring our minds to rest in the glory of the Divine Truth. May Truth inspire our reflections.

Neither non-being nor being was as yet, Neither was there death nor immortality, nor was there any sign then of night or day; totally windless, by itself, the One breathed; Beyond that, indeed nothing whatever was. Who really knows, who could here proclaim whence this creation flows, where is its origin? Who therefore knows from where it did arise? He alone in the Highest heaven, He alone knows . . . unless . . . He knows it not."

These words of the Persian divine child, Zoroaster, were written over a century BEFORE the creation story of *Genesis,* according to scholars. Zoroaster was the more lyric. "O Ahura Mazda, this I ask of thee: speak to me truly. Who establishes the sunlit days and the star glistening sphere and the Milky Way? Who, apart from thee, established the law by which the moon waxes and wanes? Who made the waters and the plants? Who yoked the two swift ones, thunder and lightning, to the wind and to the clouds? Who shaped prized love with power?"

This, of course, is only a very small segment. You may want to read the entire creation account. Truth and Beauty stand on their own feet, wherever they are found. All of the great religious traditions have pointed toward truths.

"Bow down and worship . . . where others kneel," said Ramakrishna. Christian Biblical provincialism is archaic in this age of intercontinental ballistic missiles.

Did Jesus Really
Say Those Things?

My wife and I recently returned from a joyous trip to California visiting our son, his wife, and our two grandsons. Of special interest to me was an extensive article in a Sunday edition of the *San Francisco Examiner*. Thirty of the nation's Biblical scholars, including the Dean of the Memorial Church of Stanford University, are concluding a five-year study of the New Testament. They've met at universities around the country including the University of Redlands, near San Bernardino.

They are now ready to publish their work.

The opening paragraph in the *Examiner* sets the tone: "Thirty of the nation's top biblical scholars have some bad news for Christians who still believe that the New Testament is the word of God."

Ministers do not talk about it, and the person in the pew does not know about it, but for decades now it's been common knowledge among scholars from theological schools and the religion departments of major universities that a great many of the sayings attributed to Jesus were put into his mouth by early church leaders. They did so for political reasons, theological purposes, and ecclesiastical power.

Why the five-year study? The chairman, Dr. Robert Funk, professor of religious studies at the University of Montana, explains: "For too long now, television evangelists and fundamentalists have played on the fears and ignorance of the uninformed. It is time for biblical scholars to quit the classroom and speak out. To learn that the Jesus of the Gospel of John is nothing but a figment of the evangelist's pious imagination, or that Paul is not the author of the pastoral Epistles goes down poorly with ecclesiastical officials who are more concerned with church membership and the collection plate than with historical truth."

Of more than passing interest is the following: Several men from evangelical schools were invited to participate in the seminar. They accepted. They were told by their schools to "shut up, quit the seminar or be fired." They chose to be fired, to maintain their personal and academic integrity. They were also kicked out of the Evangelical Theological Society.

The officials of their schools who threatened them are much like the priests of Galileo's day who refused to look through his telescope for fear of what they might see. How many today choose to live with a similar attitude?

I must admit that I find this public honesty now from eminent biblical scholars more than satisfying. I have been saying the same thing for at least 25 years, and only waiting for the recognized scholars to finally speak out. They plan to conclude their five-year project with a new edition of the New Testament.

I say "Thank God," we finally have scholars telling the public things that their ministers might never tell them for fear of controversy, being fired, losing money in the collection plate, or ecclesiastical shunning.

It is long, long past due for some academic integrity in the pulpit. Maybe the time has finally arrived.

What is the PURPOSE of a church?:
"The purpose is that it should be a fountainhead and dispensing center for religious thought. It should stand as a beaconlight to the world's religious perplexities. It should be a strong agency for the NEW order of things."

> *— said 80 years ago*
> *by Dr. John McLean, President,*
> *Pacific School of Religion*

The Sexuality of Jesus

The Sexuality of Christ in the Renaissance Art and in Modern Oblivion received rave reviews from all quarters. It was written by Leo Steinberg, who originally delivered the material at a Lionel Trilling Seminar at Columbia University and was honored by the College Art Association of America with its annual award. But some will find it offensive — those who find all expressions of sexuality offensive.

The sexuality of Jesus is very obvious in the paintings. Jesus was a Hebrew male, a man in the fullest sense and a sexual human being in the same sense that all men are sexual human beings.

And yet, for some strange, neurotic and weird reason, many want to keep this subject behind drawn shades or else locked in the closet. Many times, in study groups and seminars, when I have presented material that would indicate that Jesus was either married or had a mistress, there has been a tensing up and then after thinking it over — a gradual relaxing with the subject.

Even Martin Luther faced this issue squarely, saying in his *Tabletalk* that Jesus probably had sexual relations with Mary Magdalene as well as "other women." That Luther was a pretty gutsy guy. (He also wrote: "If your wife is cold, call the maid.")

Of course, Luther was not alone in his robust attitude toward sexuality. Pope Julius II by a papal decree established a "sacred" brothel in Rome that flourished under his successors, Leo X and Clement VII. The earnings of the brothel supported the Holy Sisters of the Order of St. Mary Magdalen. (Church history is not as dull as you might think.)

But back to the sexuality of Jesus.

Ancient Judaism, at his time, valued married life highly. They disdained celibacy. Every man took marriage seriously. There are no instances of life-long celibacy in the entire Old Testament, the Apocrypha, the Qumran scrolls, the Mishnah or the Talmud.

Our 20th century sexual liberalism is not the issue here. What is the issue are the sexual attitudes of first-century Judaism — and it is recorded that Jesus traveled around the countryside in intimate companionship with a group of women, including Mary Magdalene.

His entourage included "women who ministered unto him of their substance" (Luke 8:1-3). His women followers remained faithful to him right through to the end. (As compared with Judas and Peter, for instance.) And our New Testament Gospels say that only Mary Magdalene and her women attended the tomb of Jesus.

The duty of becoming betrothed shortly after puberty was axiomatic in ancient Judaism. Marriage was a religious duty that every man took seriously, and the Gospel of Mary, discovered in Egypt, leaves no doubt about the matter, suggesting that Jesus and Mary Magdalene were married.

In the Gnostic Gospel of Philip, one part reads as follows: "There were three who walked with Jesus at all times, Mary, her sister Salome and Magdalene, the who is called his partner." In another sentence, Mary Magdalene is referred to as the "spouse" of Jesus, and tells how he kisses her often.

The treasure of Gnostic gospels, discovered only as recently as 35 years ago, have many references to the sexuality of Jesus. Professor Helmut Koester of Harvard University writes that the collection of sayings in some of the Gnostic gospels may include traditions even older than the Gospels of our New Testament.

And in the Gospel of Philip are these words: "The companion of Jesus is Mary Magdalene. Jesus loved her more than all the disciples and used to kiss her often on the mouth. Jesus said to the other disciples, 'Why do I not love you as I love her?'"

This is not such a new theme, really. D. H. Lawrence and Nikos Kazantsakis made the issue of Jesus' sexuality central to two of their works. And of course one of the most haunting and beautiful songs to come out of "Jesus Christ, Superstar" was the tender rendition of "I Don't Know How to Love Him," sung by Mary Magdalene to Jesus.

The Sexuality of Christ in Renaissance Art introduces readers to a very legitimate dimension of Jesus, the man who was fully human. Many will find it refreshing.

Fundamentalist Ignorance

I was going to let fundamentalism die a natural death until I read a column last week. And my goodness sakes alive! (as my grandmother used to say). Any religious movement that is so out of harmony with contemporary science, anthropology, archaeology, astronomy, biology and higher literary criticism has no other choice than the death throes of their own "ghost dance."

Webster's New Collegiate Dictionary (1973) defines fundamentalism in these words: "a 20th century Protestant movement emphasizing a *literally* interpreted *Bible*, strict *literal* adherence."

Those scholars named in the column by the fundamentalist writer must be turning over in their graves to think that they were identified with such nonsense; Martin Luther was talking and writing about the "mythology" of the *Bible* 500 years ago; Pascal and Kierkegaard would be appalled at a literal biblical interpretation.

This sentence in the column did it: "The issue is, in reality, whether or not one takes the *Bible seriously*. If we do, we will affirm the traditional doctrines of the church."

My only regret is that I cannot type 50 pages responding to such nonsense. What "traditional doctrine?" That of Christian Science, Seventh-day Adventists, Mormons, the Gnostics, Christian Mystics, Pentacostals, Roman Catholics, Jehovah's Witnesses, Unity and Unitarian?

The quagmire of "Christian" groups, sects and denominations that now confront us make it impossible to gain any kind of consensus among "Christians" as to the meaning of any respective doctrine. The very obvious fact is that it is *doctrinal disagreement* that has created more than 400 Protestant groups, not counting Roman Catholics.

Again, according to the column, "only those who affirm the traditional doctrines take the *Bible* seriously." What he is saying is that all of the thousands of eminent biblical and religious scholars in the world who are not fundamentalists and do not read the *Bible* literally are not taking it seriously. Such a statement defies intelligent and rational thought.

He is saying that highly respected theological seminaries all across this country in the Methodist, Congregational, Presbyterian and Episcopalian (and other) denominations are not taking the *Bible* seriously. He is saying that Christian and religious scholars in the religion departments of hundreds of schools and universities are not taking the *Bible* seriously, as they are light years away from fundamentalism and repulsed by it.

He is saying that the 127 scholars from all over the world that put together *The Interpreters Bible*, a 12-volume exegetical work, have not taken the *Bible* seriously. He is saying that the following pre-eminent biblical scholars whose names are a household world to every serious student of Christianity and religion have never taken the *Bible* seriously, for none of them would even come close to affirming fundamentalism: Albert Schweitzer, Carl Jung, Joseph Campbell, Mircea Eliade, William Fox Albright, Frank Cross, George Ernest Wright, Rudolf Bultmann, Paul Tillich, Ernest Colwell, Henry Sloan Coffin, John Knox, Vincent Taylor, Frederick Grant, Edgar Goodspeed, Walter Russell Bowie. As the list would be endless, it is enough to observe that anyone saying none of these scholars took the *Bible* seriously had better drastically improve their reading list and study habits.

As the column author rightly confirmed in his last paragraph, he has chosen the way of the fundamentalists. I most certainly have not. I choose the finest scholarship available, from *all* disciplines, that throws new light upon the *Bible,* creeds, dogma and religious beliefs.

Dr. James Bennet Pritchard, professor emeritus of religious studies at the University of Pennsylvania and biblical adviser to the *National Geographic Magazine,* the British Broadcasting System and Time-Life books, and past president of the Archeological Institute of America gives us our final word:

"Discoveries have been made and reported by honest and scholarly men and women. We can never again read the *Bible* as did our grandfathers and great-grandfathers. An angel with the flaming sword of knowledge blocks the way of ever returning."

Examinations for Sunday School Teachers

It is of great interest to me that some states are now requiring examinations for teacher certification in our public schools. That is as it should be. Doctors, lawyers, as well as ministers in some major denominations must take examinations prior to practicing their profession. The thought came to me, dreamer that I am, what if Sunday school teachers had to take examinations before being allowed to influence the minds and emotions of the young?

Not too many years ago, in a remarkable editorial, the *Wall Street Journal* made the observation that we are "a nation of religious illiterates." We ask: "How can this be, considering all of the millions in Sunday schools around this country each week?"

After my second year of teaching in the religion department of the University of Puget Sound in Tacoma, I found myself increasingly appalled at the religious illiteracy of the students. I asked the chairman of the department, Dr. Richard Overman, if my classes were unusual. His reply: "Bill, I have been teaching here for 28 years, and I still find it just beyond belief that these students can reach this University so untouched by learning, with most of them having 14 years or so of Sunday schools and sermons."

Well, if we are a nation of religious illiterates, even with millions attending Sunday schools and listening to sermons, it does raise some serious questions that need to be addressed. So, please allow me to dream.

What would it be if Sunday school teachers had to take a competency and proficiency examination prior to being allowed to influence the minds and spirits of our cherished youth? I am not addressing that very, very small minority of teachers who do make every major effort to become thoroughly knowledgeable in the subject matter. I am speaking to all of those thousands who, lazily, do nothing more than pass on "what Mama told them about the Bible," the blind leading the blind, and worse.

It would take 10 pages to list questions that should be asked to determine competency in the field of teaching religion. But, a few samples:

• Discuss the role played by oral tradition in religious ritual and religious literature.

• Discuss the role of mythology in religious ritual and religious literature.

• Discuss the difference between the religion of Jesus and the theology about Jesus created by the early church.

- What are the origins of the two creation myths in Genesis? Why do they contradict each other?
- What was the influence of the Greek mystery religions on Paul's theology? Give examples.
- Why do scholars say that Christianity is saturated with Zoroastrianism? Discuss the influence of Zoroastrian mythology in Christian mythology, with example.
- Name at least two other great religious traditions with virgin birth and resurrection stories similar to those in the Christian tradition.

We are being bombarded today with the voices of those who cry, scream and yell about how important religion is, so surely learned and competent Sunday school teachers should be a high priority, you would think, in this land of "religious illiterates." Think of this: In every other major academic discipline, history, chemistry, math, etc., the students continue on in their growth to more knowledge through the exposure to scholars in the university community. Whereas, in religion classes at the university level of education, probably 95 percent of what they have been "taught" in their hometown Sunday school has to be unlearned so they can get a fresh start with scholars in all phases of religious studies, scholars who have spent a lifetime of study and research in their field.

It is truly a preposterous dilemma. Sunday school teachers required to take competency examinations for certification. Ah, what a dreamer am I.

Ritualist Cannabalism . . . Communion

When I was teaching at the University of Puget Sound one of the sections of the course was an exploration of the religious rituals of primal peoples and the vestiges of those rituals that we still observe and practice today.

One of the more obvious rituals was the "sacred meal," or cannibalism. Following that part of the course, some of the students would always ask me to explain how I could serve communion and still participate in that ancient ritual. I told them I could do it easily, by placing it within a different context and using different language, which I will say more about at the end of this column.

The sacred meal is a familiar and common theme in religions. The communicant eats and drinks, symbolically or literally, the flesh and the blood of the divine "leader." Derivatives and vestiges of these are obviously found today in the Protestant and Catholic Communion.

For example, the traditional invitation to Communion, spoken by the presiding clergy, is this: "Take, eat, this is my body . . . this cup is the new covenant in my blood, this do as often as you drink it, in remembrance of me." Eating a body and drinking blood is a cannibalistic theme, even if it is symbolic cannibalism.

One anthropological scholar who has spent a lifetime studying this ritual is Dr. Jean-Paul Dumont, professor of anthropology at the University of Washington. He writes: "Cannibalism has always been a part of religious behavior. The principle remains the same . . . acquiring through ingestion the powers of something, whether human or divine. The purpose has always been to take on the qualities of the person being eaten. It has most always been an act of respect and honor.

Through the ritual you inherit the qualities and share in the divinity of the one being eaten. It was a triumph of life over death. In our Christian traditions we are still practicing this ritual in a symbolic form."

Now for the question of how can I serve and participate in the ritual of communion so that it has significance and is in the spirit of the One who said, "Follow thou me?"

I do not use the cannibalistic words about eating a body and drinking blood, but treat it as a fellowship breaking bread together and sharing the memory and the spirit of Jesus. Breaking bread together and drinking wine have been a sign of fellowship, of shared memories, shared faith and hope for thousands of years.

Bread for thousands of years has been a symbol of strength, spiritual food and truth. Wine has been a symbol for life and wisdom. Says the Hebrew Qabbalah, "it is the symbol for the mysterious vitality and spiritual energy of all created things."

There is a beautiful teaching in Judaism that says Abraham went to see his great-grandfather Shem, and Shem gave him bread and wine. Shem's message to Abraham was that if you want to turn the world to God, you have to give them bread and wine; the old must be connected to the new and fresh and vital. Bread is best when it's fresh. With wine, the older it is, the more beautiful it is.

And so we quite simply "take" bread and wine together as a community united with those gone before and those still with us. We remember the spirit of the One who said "follow thou me" and whose spirit lives on and whose memory we celebrate in a shared meal around a table.

There is a tragedy in the Christian church, never better expressed than by Samual Driver, when he was professor of Hebrew at Oxford University.

"There is nothing more tragic in the history of the Christian church than the fact that its central ritual has for centuries been, and still is, a subject for the most intense hatred and fighting. Christians have been put to death, cruel deaths, by other Christians for not believing the same doctrines about the Lord's Supper, which cannot be proved, and which are possibly not even true. The sacrament of Love has been made a sacrament of hate and destruction, because men have insisted that they possessed knowledge which cannot be possessed . . . and have tried to explain what cannot be explained."

Surely, when bread (strength) and wine (life, vitality and spiritual energy) are shared together by a community of faith, hope and love, in memory of His spirit, nothing more need be said; nothing more need be added.

God Type Power . . .
Church Bishops

How would you like to have been a bishop, or a priest, or even a deacon back in the first several hundred years after Jesus died — back when the Christian Church was forming its political structure?

You would have had power, with a capital "P" — God-type power. Whoever refused to "bow the neck" to the bishops, wrote Clement, Bishop of Rome, would get an ax — like POW!

The bishop "stands in the place of God," and you had to "obey the bishop as if he were God," wrote Bishop Ignatius of Antioch.

With power like that — with everyone bowing down and sending in their bucks — you would be living on the fat of the land. (We used to call it "hog heaven" down in Texas.)

How do you keep that kind of power, with all those peons bowing down to you and sending in their bucks?

It's easy. You just have to convince them that only you can get them into some place called "heaven," reminding them constantly of the alternative, some place called "hell." (This practice still is in use by many Christian churches.)

You have to convince the people that when they die that's it; they never are coming back to Earth, and either heaven or hell are waiting for them. Then you have to sell them the great bottom line con job — that only through you, the bishop and the church can they get into heaven.

That kind of stuff, when believed by the poor guy down the street, makes Oral Roberts seeing his 900-foot Jesus and doing a stint on God's death row pale by comparison. Oral is just not thinking big enough. He should read how the bishops and clergy did it in the first several centuries.

Are you ready for the next episode? Along came a group of people called Gnostics. Do you know what they had the brazen gall to preach?

They said: "Folks, we don't need bishops and priests and clergy. We don't need this political structure called the 'church.' Every person can, by himself or herself, approach God."

You can just imagine how that went over with the bishops with their flowing velvet robes and overflowing collection plates.

"That is heresy," they cried, "heresy! Kill them all."

That isn't all. More nice people are going to get the ax. Almost everyone back then believed in reincarnation. But what if you were a bishop, and some smart aleck said: "You can't get me into a place called heaven, because I'm coming back again in the karmic cycle, and you ain't got nothing to do with it."

With that kind of thinking around, any bishop with an IQ above 5 could see all his power going right down the drain. So, what do you do?

You could just proclaim that reincarnation is also an evil — "heresy" — and that anyone who believes it, or talks about it, is going to get the big ax.

And so, in the year 553 A.D., the Second Council of Constantinople (a group of men losing control) declared that belief in reincarnation was heresy. Between the 12th and 16th century, thousands upon thousands of so-called Christian 'heretics' who believed in reincarnation were put to death by order of the Roman Catholic inquisitions.

The great and brilliant minds who believe in reincarnation — including Goethe, Einstein and Nobel Prize physicists — number in the thousands. (I'll write more on that later.)

The church today still is loaded down with clergy and priests with sixth-century mentalities. They would like to brand all such thought as "heresy." They would like to have said to Einstein as to Galileo, "You are a heretic."

If the church and clergy lose control over who gets into "heaven," how they get there, what you're supposed to believe to get there . . . If more and more people finally realize that they don't need the church, or the clergy, to get them there . . . the jig's up, as you can plainly see.

Congregations with Frontal Lobotomies

Recently I received a long distance telephone call from an embarrassed member of the hospice group in a prominent Idaho community. The group had invited me to lead a two-day seminar comparing the world's major religious traditions, emphasizing different views on death and dying, which is what the hospice program is all about. The seminar was to be held in one of the local churches.

An officer of that church decided he had better find out what I was going to say. I told him about the material that I would be presenting. He informed me that the congregation recently had allowed a speaker to come in who talked about "astrology" and all of that "occult stuff" and they would not allow any of that kind of thing in their church.

Then came the call from the hospice member to tell me that the church officers had decided they did not want a "controversial" speaker coming into their church to talk about all of those "foreign" religions and things. (Someone should inform them that Christianity is a "foreign" religion, and the only native American religion is that of the North American Indians.)

What a church like that needs is obviously all of the fresh air that it can possibly let in. The fact is, you don't know what you think until you hear someone who thinks differently. Any church that cuts itself off from such dialogue and from mental and spiritual stimulation becomes smug and stupid and completely incapable of defending its own beliefs, except by dogma.

Every church, in order to stay vigorous and spiritually alive, should have a dozen "outside" speakers a year. And the speakers should be as "outside" as they can get — from Zen masters to agnostics, anthropologists and physicists. This is a marvelous way to awaken an impotent congregation suffering from sleeping sickness. The rather pathetic commentary on all of this is that the majority of the time the "outside" speaker knows a hundred times more about the *Bible*, Christianity and religion than those barring the doors to them.

One of the most prestigious awards in America is given annually by the Templeton Foundation for "Progress in Religion." (John Templeton, a Presbyterian layman, founded the award in 1973.) The recipients have distinguished themselves in spiritual endeavors.

The 1985 winner of the $185,000 award is Sir Allister Hardy of Oxford University. He has spent a lifetime studying human spiritual experiences. In his acceptance speech, he said that he feels, without any question, that human spirituality is evolving into a higher consciousness. But, he continued, "I do not think that there is any future at all for orthodox Christian beliefs and dogma . . . because they refuse to realize that all of the great religious traditions are part of the same God."

In a remarkable address to the graduating class of Princeton University theological seminary a few years ago, Dr. Samuel Miller, dean of the theological seminary of Harvard University said: "Orthodox Christianity is very close to death's door. The churches are addressing themselves in a dead language to situations and issues that no longer exist. The patterns of truth are different. The questions have new terms. Nothing could be more tragic than to find ourselves hugging our own sanctified, false Christian idols, blind and hostile to the living revelation of God's mystery in our own time. The Christianity that is interested only in its institution and ecclesiastical niceties is worse than vanity, it is incestuous."

Any Christian church closing its doors and its mind to "outside" speakers is not only impotent, but spiritually bankrupt. I am glad the officers refused to allow the seminar, because it might prove to be a genuine learning experience and a shattering eye opener to some of the more open, enlightened and searching members of that congregation.

Another major church in that same community offered the hospice group their facilities and welcomed the seminar with joy, open doors and open arms.

Sanctuary, Pulpit and Courtrooms

Think about this: The typical church service in a typical sanctuary on a typical Sunday morning bears a striking resemblance to a court of law. The minister has on a similar gown, most often black. The pews and pulpit closely resemble the furniture of a courtroom. The minister is elevated above the audience.

The minister preaches law from that idol that has replaced God, called the Bible. The audience (subjects) are supposed to symbolically prostrate themselves before all of this. The judge (minister) interprets the law.

No wonder it is so difficult, if not almost impossible, to think your way beyond all of these trappings to the enlightenment of a higher religious consciousness, especially if you have been subjected to this kind of an authoritarian atmosphere since early childhood.

It is no wonder that archaic and idolatrous images of God are so hard to change, or even examine with an open mind. Few seem to realize that clinging desperately to images of God is the very opposite of living in faith. Faith is a condition of being open. It is trust. When you swim, you relax and trust yourself to the water. You don't cling to the water, or get uptight and fight the water or you sink. In like manner, one who clings to certain creeds, doctrines and propositions about God, Jesus and the creation, is one who has no faith at all.

To trust in a mystery that is beyond human comprehension, imagination, definition or description is a far, far higher form for faith than clinging to idolatrous images and definite conceptions of something that we call God.

You probably remember the story of the little child who wanted so much to hold and keep the beautiful butterfly in his hand. He clutched his fist tightly around it so that it would not get away. By so doing he crushed it. In his clinging, he killed it.

Faith is not clinging to anything of the Spirit, for in clinging we lose it. You cannot cling to water for it will slip through your fingers. If you cling to your breath, you will turn purple and die. The Buddhist word nirvana means to "breathe out," to "let go." Letting go is an act of faith. Jesus told Mary Magdalene in the book of John, "Don't cling to me."

The Spirit flows, and like wind and water, when you try to tighten your fist around it, it slips through your fingers and you have lost it or crushed it.

The most honest and humble statement that we can make as we stand before the mystery that is beyond human comprehension is the "I do not know" of agnosticism. That is a statement of faith, free of the images created by human beings.

This is not a new thought. Perhaps the basic source book of Christian spirituality is the *Theologia Mystica*, written in the sixth century by an Assyrian monk, Dionysius Exiguus. It explains that the highest knowledge of God is through agnostos (unknowing). This says that we know God in the most profound sense by, in faith, admitting that we do not know; therefore we have no images. It is to cease clinging to superstitious conceptions. To paraphrase James Joyce, "It is, in faith, to forge an uncreated spiritual conscience of the race."

Faith is a conscience that is not handed down ready-made from Mount Sinai, or the Sermon on the Mount, despite all of those who would like for us to believe otherwise. It is not just simply a matter of clearing out the debris from an ancient age — dead forms, defunct symbols, and myths that have become lifeless — for it means to defy the institutional gods, even as Prometheus in his own day defied Hercules.

The unknowable mystery, flowing through every call of our bodies and dancing in cosmic rhythms, is beyond our comprehension. That mystery within us waits to be brought forth and converted into a source of more light for the fulfillment of human destiny . . . in our own time.

"God does not die on the day when we cease to believe in a personal deity, but we die on the day when our lives cease to be illumined by the steady radiance . . . renewed daily . . . of a wonder . . . the source of which is beyond all reason."

— Dag Hammarskjold

"God does not exist. He is being itself beyond essence and existence. Therefore, to argue that God 'exists' is to deny Him."

— Paul Tillich

The Need for Kindred Spirits

I have lost count of the times that somebody has said to me: "I don't have any more need for institutional religion. I have outgrown all of that Sunday morning stuff. I can find it on my own."

Well, what they are missing is the sharing with others who come together once a week for a renewed confirmation of who and what they are as a religious community.

There is a unique, rich and rewarding relationship that can develop each Sunday morning between the pulpit and the pew. What happens is something that cannot take place anywhere else in our daily lives, not on the golf course or in a fishing stream, in Rotary or any other kind of civic and social organization.

An enormous amount of personal and spiritual growth can take place in a church where both the pulpit and pew cherishes freedom — the freedom to doubt, to question, to be honest in the search for those religious values that enrich our lives in daily living — and where there's the belief that religion does not have to be wedded to nonsense and absurdity.

The Sunday morning hour can be a beautiful time for spiritual growth and insights when certain elements are present.

There is a pulpit and a "preacher," talking, talking, talking week after week, month after month and year after year. Does the man or the woman in the pulpit speak truly, as they know life, understand it and have experienced it? Does the person in the pulpit have integrity, academic and personal? Is he or she the "real stuff," as Carl Jung put it?

Is the person in the pulpit refusing to play the games that so many play for salary raises and promotions? Does the person in the pulpit have the courage to, week after week, expose honestly mind, heart and soul, doubts and questions, joys and angers? Does he or she have that kind of courage and integrity? Is he real bones and flesh, spirit and matter, mind and heart?

I'm not talking about beauty of language, grace of composition or brilliance of presentation. I'm talking about a man or a woman speaking about things that are very important to him or her — not trying to entertain, make an impression or tell you what you would like to hear, but speaking plainly from the heart.

And then there's the listener in the pew who has come to share in this weekly experience.

How did you go to that worship service on any given Sunday? What attitudes did you bring? Did you bring a certain frame of mind for this hour — an openness to absorb whatever viable seed is cast on this particular morning?

Nothing can ever take place in the pew for those who go to judge in a trivial and superficial way, or to appraise the sermon, the style, the theme, whether it is old or new, whether it has been covered before or never in recent memory.

When you go free of judgments, with an open mind and spirit, something can happen that is more wonderful, enriching, growth producing and stimulating than at any alter practicing magical religious rituals or at any doctrinal pulpit reciting magical verbal formulas and creedal cliches.

There's another dimension. It's something that has to do with that person sitting next to you. We need to know that we belong to, and share with others those ideas and those things that we treasure, that we are a part of a community sharing a similar spiritual journey, that there are others who feel as we do.

We need to know that. We need to feel that support, encouragement and affection. And so we come together once a week for a renewed confirmation of who and what we are as a community. People who cannot, or do not, experience something like that are missing something terribly important.

Ministers are NOT Bible Scholars

The gap between the *Bible* as viewed by biblical scholars and as viewed by Mr. and Mrs. John Doe of the First Church of Green River, Kansas . . . or Big Tree, Washington, . . . or Little Tree, California, . . . or whatever . . . is a gap that leaves one in a state of bewilderment . . . and sometimes shock.

Let me say a word about biblical scholars. The vast majority of ministers are NOT biblical scholars. I'm not. I must depend on top scholars who have the highest academic credentials.

Most ministers have rather been indoctrinated only with what their particular denomination wanted them to propagate and sustain. And 95 percent of ministers, who are called "Dr." are not really doctors at all . . . and have not earned either a doctor's degree or a Ph.D. The doctorate is an honorary Doctorate of Divinity, presented usually by some small church college in their own denomination . . . or else it can be bought from any number of small, non-accredited schools for 25 bucks.

I want to define biblical scholar. When I use that term, I am referring to those scholars who are studied and are looked upon as competent authorities in the departments of religion in our major universities in the world, or major theological seminaries. I am not talking about someone in some small denominational seminary somewhere who must repeat the party line to hold his job.

But now let's get closer to home — the churches.

Here is a Methodist minister, a Presbyterian minister, an Episcopalian, or whatever. He tries to keep abreast of the latest scholarship . . . he studies . . . he returns to a university periodically for a sabbatical. Now, what happens is this . . . in maybe 90 percent of the churches . . . he returns to his pulpit . . . and begins to bring to the congregation what he has learned. And what happens? The John Doe's of the congregation rise up in arms with a vengeance. "What does he mean saying those things about our *Bible?*

"He's not going to get away with saying those things. We'll get a new minister who will tell us what we want to hear . . . what our mamas told us about the *Bible*."

Don't think for one minute I am exaggerating. I AM NOT. The senior minister of one of our largest churches said these words to me, "I just say sweet things Sunday after Sunday that the folks like to hear, Edelen . . . that's just good politics."

I know ministers who have continued studying. They know better than the things they are saying on Sunday morning, but they cannot lose their jobs. They have children to feed and clothe, and they have bills; maybe they are not trained for anything else . . . they cannot afford to lose their jobs . . . even for academic and intellectual integrity.

And so they swallow hard and continue saying what the John Doe's of their congregation want to hear. Would you not do that, too in their shoes? What would you do? You have a growing family . . . you have a degree from Harvard . . . or Chicago . . . You know the best scholarship, but you have bills to pay . . . you have a congregation that wants to read the *Bible* as their grandmother read it. And so you do not bring to your congregation the latest research, studies, findings, writings, of the scholars in religion . . . Christianity . . . or the *Bible*.

This is no exaggeration. And that is exactly why we are in this incongruous situation we are in in the Christian church — (1) that a very small percentage of ministers have come from theological seminaries where a really top-flight education has been possible or presented, and (2) that those ministers who have been exposed to topflight education must hold it back and repress it in order to hold a church who wants to hear only what mama told them about the *Bible*.

"To thine ownself be true, and it must follow as the night the day, thou canst not then be false to any man."

— Shakespeare

"What do you suppose it takes to satisfy the soul . . . but to walk free and have no superior."

— Walt Whitman

"I challenged ALL axioms."

— Albert Einstein

The Pulpit Needs Agnostics

For more than 25 years the beloved Senior Minister of the famed City Temple of London (Methodist) was Leslie Weatherhead. His books have been read by millions.

In the *Christian Agnostic* he opens with this: "Not for much longer will the world put up with the lies, the superstitions and the distortions with which the simple message of Jesus has been overlaid. The message of Galilee has been so overlaid with creeds, ceremonies and doctrines, that one can hardly catch the essential message."

He goes on to say that any minister, standing in a pulpit, who is not an agnostic is dangerous. Why is he (she) dangerous? Because he pretends to have positive and absolute answers, that he does not have. He lives in the 20th century, parroting back a third century biblical mentality, as though nothing had been learned, thought or discovered in the last 1700 years.

As the religious historian Joseph Campbell put it: "The majority of ministers either do not understand their material or else are deliberately misrepresenting it, if they know better. They present myth and metaphor as historical, literal events. The idea of virgin birth, for example, is presented as historical fact, whereas every mythology (and religious tradition) in the world has included the mythological motif of virgin birth in their legends and folklore. American Indian mythologies abound in virgin births."

I commend his latest book to those of you who would like to become more knowledgeable in this area. It is *The Inner Reaches of Outer Space*.

What these scholars are telling us is this: There was a Jesus of history with a simple message. Then there is the 'Christ' mythology created by the early church, using well-known mythological themes of Babylon, Egypt, Persia and Greece. For several hundred years, for instance, early Christians in Alexandria would worship before statues of the Holy Virgin, the Holy Mother Isis. She was suckling her divine child, Horus, whom she had conceived miraculously.

In April 1985 there was an International Symposium held at the University of Michigan in Ann Arbor. Distinguished scholars from major universities in Europe and America presented papers on the Jesus of history and the Jesus of mythology.

Gerald Larue, professor of biblical history, University of Southern California, said this: "Writers put in Jesus' mouth what the early church wanted him to say. For clergy who know better, why are they not communicating to their parishioners what they know? For clergy who do not know any better, it is simply a matter of ignorance."

Van A. Harvey, professor of religion, Stanford University, used these words: "Anyone teaching Christianity, or the *Bible*, to college students cannot help but be struck by the enormous gap between what the average layperson thinks is historical truth about Jesus, and what the great majority of biblical scholars know after a century and a half of research."

Let it be said that there are ministers keeping their congregations abreast of the latest scholarship in religious studies. The largest Congregational church in America (United Church of Christ), the denomination to which I belong, is the Church of the Beatitudes in Phoenix, Arizona. The Senior Minister there made this observation in a December sermon: "The key to Renaissance thought is the questioning spirit and the willingness to entertain doubt (agnosticism).

"I have no use," he said, "for any religion that does not liberate the human mind to ask great questions. I am impatient with any religion which dampens the inquisitive spirit in humans. I am appalled by any religion that pretends to have firm, final and absolute answers."

Weatherhead gives us our final reminder: "Any minister, standing in a pulpit, who is not an agnostic, is dangerous."

PRAYER

Can Requests Change God's Will?

I would like to ask, "Can something called God's will really be changed by requests from the earth?" And, if so, "What kind of a capricious, chaotic universe would this be?"

The Encyclopedia Britannica says that belief in an unchangeable God or unchangeable force is to be found in all of the higher religions.

Jesus is credited with saying that God makes his rain fall on the just and the unjust alike, the sun to shine on the just and the unjust alike.

What kind of chaos would it be if the eternal will, the eternal God, the eternal design could be changed from time to time as this design was subjected to millions of people in a barrage of requests to make things different?

It is incomprehensible to me how such thought can be entertained. It is the type of thinking done by Eddie Rickenbacker and crew, as expressed after their rescue from an ocean raft in the South Pacific. They uttered desperate prayers for rescue and, when a ship did finally appear, full credit was given God.

Do you know what bothers me terribly? When I think with aching heart of all the thousands of good and fine men who desperately croaked out words of urgent appeal to God through parched and anguished throats and whose answer was to be devoured by shark and barracuda, to die from starvation or drowning.

Why were there no miracles performed by God in order to save them? Were they less good, less virtuous, less sincere than Rickenbacker? How could anyone worship a God who was so capricious as to save Rickenbacker and let thousands die horrible deaths, including those in Nazi gas chambers? What kind of God could this be? What kind of God could allow us to believe such nonsense?

"If God is God, he is not good. If God is good, he is not God. Take the even, take the odd," wrote Archibald MacLeish in the play *J.B.*

Well, there is a massive cop-out in thinking this question through seriously. And the massive cop-out is to come up with the lame answer that God heard the prayers, but the answer was no. God says, "No, you must go ahead and get chewed up by a shark. It will be a learning experience for someone."

Do you realize how many prayers consist of pleading with God to deviate from the natural laws of the universe; to alter the rhythm and to perform religious magic because of the merit, the eloquence, the sincerity of the one doing the requesting?

"Faith" healing raises many questions, for it implies that natural law may be superseded and that miracles may be performed for the faithful. Now, I am not saying for one minute that healings do not take place.

I am not only asking, "Does a God, or supernatural force have anything to do with it, or is it a matter of natural law?" If the mind can make you sick, changes in the mind and attitude can make you well again.

A God so capricious as to heal some and permit others to suffer the most horrible pains would hardly be worthy of the attributes of love and compassion. If a supernatural being would intercede and restore health to a sick person as a result of verbal requests hurled his way, then how are we to account for the thousands of good and God-loving people who suffer painfully?

If you believe that God hears some and rejects others, then it presents to you quite frankly the most tortuous problem about the mercy and love of God. If you really believe that God heals those at so-called sacred shrines such as Lourdes (those who touch and bathe in the waters), then what about those who do not have the money to make such an expensive trip to Lourdes?

Are we to assume that a God of love and mercy will allow a child to come down with leukemia simply because the parents of that child, or the child, did not possess the necessary religious belief that would attract God's intervention?

If God is the God of the universe, then healing powers are a part of natural law and would be just as available at the corner of 9th and Main in Boise or 1st and Park Streets in McCall, Idaho, as at Lourdes.

Does God play favorites and limit his own powers of healing to specific locations and places? Who could believe in such a capricious deity?

When we spell the name of God with the wrong alphabet blocks like kindergarten children, we form childish words and infantile concepts that impede the intelligent quest for the divine mystery and the mature faith.

In our search for the right alphabet blocks to spell the name of God — ignorance, magic, sorcery, superstition, threats, fear, and supernatural caprice — must be deleted from the alphabet of divinity.

Prayer and Magic

In the study of religion and anthropology among primal peoples you find that many believed in "magic." Magic is defined as the belief that supernatural forces can be controlled, influenced and manipulated by executing a ritualistic formula, either physical or verbal. We still today, in a more fashionable way, utilize superstition, prayer wheels, magic, sacrifices and elaborate doxologies to induce God to favor our requests, grant our wishes and perform miracles upon demand.

Minister, rabbi and priest are expected to offer prayers on behalf of the desires of their congregations. Does this not make God a divine magician? And does this not make the minister or priest a magician's apprentice, *if* this is your view of prayer and how to influence God.

How many times have I been asked, as every minister, "Pray for my husband, he is so ill." I say, "Certainly I will," and I do. But I think, can my prayer mean anything as compared with the depth and sincerity of a prayer the wife could articulate. What kind of a God would heed me when he had the eloquence and the passion, the need and the pourings of the heart, mind and soul of this wife who loves her ill husband so?

God has even been associated with "winning" and "success." If you know God (and Jesus) you win, and if not, you lose. Or in other words, God plays favorites. It is Roger Staubach yelling to a Jesus Fair crowd in Dallas, "I'm telling you that loving Jesus is just like a football game, you work to put yourself in scoring position. Loving Jesus puts you in a scoring position."

But then we were left hanging as to whether loving Jesus was going to be worth a three-point field goal, a six-point touchdown with a one- or two-point conversion, or what? To illustrate the absurdity further, let us imagine that the football team of John Doe State College is praying for victory 24 hours a day over their forthcoming game with the Pittsburgh Steelers. They are *never* going to beat the Steelers, even if the entire team of the Steelers are devout atheists. And suppose God actually heard a prayer from both sides to "do one's best," and took an active part in answering that prayer.

This would obviously mean that the superior person, or team, mentally and physically, would *always win*, provided both had taken time to pray, because the "best" effort of the superior team is always going to be better than the best effort of the inferior team. So you could say that God only honors the prayers of those already mentally and physically superior. Do not 90 percent of our prayers approach the absurd and appall the sensitive?

A football team goes into a "prayer huddle" prior to the kickoff and then proceeds to do such damage to human beings that some are carried off in stretchers, some are damaged for life. (I love football. It is the prayer part that is the comical and sacrilegious.)

A boxer crosses himself prior to the bout, gives his opponent a brain concussion, breaks his jaw, and then "thanks God" for the victory. People who came down with polio, even after prayer, said "God's will." But along came Salk and outwitted God. Salk's vaccine is quite obviously stronger than "God's will" and more effective than prayer.

What is the nature of prayer? It is not magic nor is it participating in ritualistic formulas aimed at placating and influencing the gods. Mature prayer enables us to gain the kind of faith described by Josiah Royce: "Faith is the discovery of a reality that enables one to face anything that can happen to one in the universe."

Mature prayer seeks to enter into communion with the divine mystery so that we might find a source of strength in a power beyond ourselves. It is a spiritual bridge, the fusion of the infinite with the finite, the calling forth of the divine mystery within you, to commune with the divine mystery beyond you.

It is George Washington Carver, when asked why he never prayed, saying, "My every moment is prayer." At its loftiest, prayer becomes contemplation, an act of adoration towards the Mystery from Whom comes the wonder of life. It is simply saying, "O Thou, before whom all words recoil."

"Prayer: It could be an attempt to relate ourselves to the unknown potentialities for good within us; to bind ourselves humbly to something bigger than we are; to probe more deeply into the significance of man's role in this universe; to catch a glimpse of the wonder and mystery and love that the word God holds within individuals."

— The Journey,
by Lilian Smith

Prayer and Celebration

I will try and put into words what prayer means to me.

Prayer is living every hour of every day absorbed in God consciousness. It is being in a sustained state of awe, adoration, wonder and celebration of the glory that is life — whether listening to beautiful music, talking with friends, reading, playing at some game in God's marvelous natural world or working at a labor of love.

Prayer is living every moment conscious that, "This is the day which God hath made, let us rejoice and be glad in it." It is experiencing the truth of the Greek oracle. "Summoned or not summoned, God is here."

Prayer is not just spasmodic spurts of piety, only before meals or before bedtime. Now, I enjoy saying words of thanksgiving sometimes before meals, but not all the time. "Man does not live by bread alone," Jesus said. And yet to watch people always just thanking God for bodily food, you would think that the most important thing God had given us was potatoes.

Have you ever seen anyone bow his or her head and offer thanksgiving just before putting on Beethoven's Ninth Symphony? Or give thanks for the marvelous minds that gave us stereophonic reproduction and magnificent music? Or for all the other forms of beauty that fill our days and feed our spirits?

Sir Thomas Browne, the great physician, used these words: "Prayer is an attitude toward life."

In the first question of the catechism, John Calvin asked, "What is the chief end of man?" His answer: "To enjoy God forever." To enjoy.

Prayer is an attitude. It is a constant reaching out in an attempt to feel union and harmony with the spirit and the rhythm that permeates and fills the universe.

Prayer is becoming saturated with great joy of God and life. It is Carl Jung saying, "I could no more live without God, than I could live without oxygen." Goethe put it this way in Faust: "Yourself must feel it first. All refreshed the soul still sickens, till from the soul itself, the fountain bursts. . . ."

This bursting fountain is a by-product of becoming intoxicated with life, with wonder and mystery. It is all festival. It is all celebration. It is a spontaneous joy that keeps us imperishably childlike and imperishably creative. It is only released when the hard crust of pseudo-sophistication, pseudo-seriousness and pseudo-dignity is finally cut away and shed.

Submerged in everydayness, we begin to treat all hours alike. The days are drab. Nights revolt in despair. All moments are stillborn. All hours seem stale. What is left is the disintegration of being human. We need to cut through the facade of sophistication and prudence. These are spiritual diseases.

To celebrate is to contemplate the uniqueness of the moment. Today will shortly be gone, never to return. What did we do with it? Every moment is a new arrival. How do we respond to this marvel in exaltation? Celebration is feeling the intoxication and the exaltation of existence day by day like a child. It is one of the rewards of being human. It is saying, "Zorba . . . teach me to dance."

This, I believe, is prayer: to learn how, once again, to dance and sing before God in the continual celebration of life. "Unless you become as a child . . . you will never experience the Kingdom," Jesus said. A child is as conscious of mystery and wonder as naturally as of the warmth of the sun or the perfume of a flower.

This concept of prayer invites us to take hold of each moment, as it presents itself and in the form in which it presents itself — whether in life or death.

"A word to those who feel that they cannot find the words of prayer and remain silent towards God. Silence is silent prayer, namely, the sighs which are too deep for words. Then He who searches the hearts of humans, knows and hears."

— *Paul Tillich (theologian)*

"At its loftiest, prayer ceases to be a petition. PRAYER BECOMES CON-TEMPLATION."

— *Dr. Alexis Carrel, M.D.*
(Nobel Prize scientist)

RELIGIOUS ISSUES

School Prayer

Politicians in our national capital proclaimed 1985 to be the Year of the Bible and endlessly extolled the "need to return to God" by prayer in public schools.

One can only wish that they would take time to blow the dust off their coffee table Bibles and read what Jesus had to say about prayer in the Sermon on the Mount: "And when you pray you must not be like the hypocrites; for they love to stand and pray in the synagogues and at the street corners, that they may be seen by men. When you pray, go into your room and shut the door and pray to God in secret."

The school prayer issue is demeaning to prayer. It degrades prayer. You cannot regulate and legislate communication with the Mystery, the Holy. Attempting to compartmentalize prayer into a two minute pre-class segment in a tax-supported public school demeans all that is sacred.

If starting the day with prayer is important to parents, they have several hours at home before the child leaves for school either to force or encourage their child to pray. But, in the home, where it rightly belongs.

The potential obscenities of prayer in public school are so obvious as to make one shudder.

An example: My roommate at McCormick Theological Seminary in Chicago had a church in a rural, fundamentalist Bible belt section of northern Indiana. His family lived there in the parsonage. His fourth grade daughter came home from school one day crying out of control. Why was she crying so? Her fundamentalist teacher had just told her she was going to burn in hell forever, because she was "lost." Now, you might ask, how did her teacher know she was "lost?" The teacher explained to my roommate that she could tell by the way his daughter acted; she did not bow her head during morning prayer, and "the look in her eyes was not right," and she might possibly be ruled by "Satan." My roommate's livid appearance before the school board accomplished nothing in that community.

The incident brings back to my mind a cartoon of several years ago in *The Idaho Statesman*. The teacher is standing up before her second or third grade class with a large ruler in her hand. On the blackboard behind her is printed "VOLUNTARY PRAYER, 8:45 a.m. OR ELSE." And the teacher is saying to her class of young innocent minds, "Class will confine its style of classroom prayer to the normal, proper, accepted, conservative, all-American, right wing, Christian variety"!

Innocent little children can be used, violated and manipulated by a "true believer" teacher. The teacher can be anywhere on a scale of religious fanaticism from one to ten.

What makes this issue all the more bizarre is that our brilliant founding fathers would be appalled at the manner in which their names are tossed around Washington, D.C., with a total misrepresentation and prostitution of their religious views. The ignorance of some of our Senators and Congressmen on this issue is embarrassing.

Our major Founding Fathers were all Deists and Freethinkers by their own admission as spelled out in papers, letters and addresses. They included George Washington, Thomas Jefferson, Benjamin Franklin, John Adams, James Madison, Thomas Paine, and yes, even Abraham Lincoln. "God" was always a "force" or "providence." They did not believe in the divinity of Jesus; they did not believe that the Bible was either revelation or sacred literature.

We can only wish that some of those politicians in Washington, D.C., who violate the religious views of our Founding Fathers, and who play footsie with the religious broadcasters, would rediscover something . . . called . . . integrity.

Abortion

I have avoided the subject of abortion and the pro-lifers. But the time has come when I feel that I would like to make some observations.

If a person wants to simply say "I do not like abortion. I am against it," that is fine. That's their opinion and they have every right to express it.

But, it is when they start using the Bible and the Church to justify and condone their pro-life position that I cringe. They apparently do not realize how inane and unhinged they appear when they march around carrying signs quoting the commandment "Thou shalt not kill," or equally absurd signs using the Church or God for justification.

After Moses told the people that the "Thou shalt not kill" order came from "God," he then proceeded to give some of the most vicious commands in the history of civilization, telling the Hebrews to kill just about everything that walked or moved.

And Moses even told them that "God" blessed all of this barbaric slaughter. He gave commands for genocide . . . to kill babies and children . . . (except the young virgins . . . the men were to keep them . . . and use them). He gave orders for a scorched earth policy . . . and thousands were slaughtered as a result of the commands of Moses.

Quite obviously, "Thou shalt not kill" *was not taken seriously by the very man who gave the commandment.* If you want to get sick to your stomach (don't read it before breakfast), open your Bible, pro-lifers, and start reading at Numbers 31:17.

As for using the Christian Church to justify the pro-life position, I would seriously suggest to those marching in the streets that they read the history of their church regarding murder, if they can stand it. The Church has one of the most horrible, unjust and cruel murder records in the history of our species, from Constantine, through the Inquisition to the Salem witch horror.

The Inquisition, started in Spain in 1233, was joined in 1478 by the Pope, run by the Holy Office, and covered all of Europe. It was not ended until 1820. For 600 years the Christian Church carried on the systematic, horrible slaughter of hundreds of thousands of innocent men and women.

The torture chambers of the "Christian" Inquisition were filled with instruments that stagger the human mind and human sensibilities: racks, thumb screws, iron maidens, knives, whips, scourges, fire, tongs and hoists. You could not bear to read how these were used on innocent human beings.

In the Inquisition all possessions had to be turned over to the Church. Families were encouraged to denounce one another. No charge was needed to be given on arrest. The accuser was the judge.

John Calvin burned Servetus at the stake because the brilliant Servetus said he could not find any evidence of the Trinity in the Gospels.

Had Jesus lived during that period, there is no question that he, too, would have been sent to the torture chambers or burned at the stake by the Christians.

And now, those using the Church and the Bible for justification of their pro-life position condemn abortion as "murder" of the "unborn," while the Church itself has a 600-year history of the most horrible and brutal murders of the "born."

I would suggest that those mindlessly waving banners in the streets read some church history, and take time to reflect on the hypocrisy of their position. If they want to say simply, "I am against abortion" and let it go at that, fine. But in the name of all that is truth, and all that is sacred, let them stop using the bloody hands of Moses and the Church for their justification.

"The Commandments of Israel are clearly savage taboos of a familiar type in primitive religions . . . disguised as commands of a deity."

— Sir James Frazier
(anthropologist)

"The Commandment against killing referred ONLY to killing another Israelite. It did NOT forbid the killing of animals . . . peoples of other nations . . . capital punishment or suicide."

— The Interpreter's Bible, Volume I

"The Commandment against bearing false witness against one's neighbor meant ONLY a brother Hebrew. They never applied this standard in their dealings with other peoples."

— Dr. Henry Sloan Coffin,
former President
Union Theological Seminary

Euthanasia

The scene is in the intensive care section of an Oklahoma hospital. The woman strapped to the bed is 84 years old. She is my mother. I am sitting beside her with my wife.

A doctor enters the room. He is called a specialist. He walks over to the old, tired, pain-racked body and says cheerfully: "Mrs. Edelen, we are going to make you as shiny and bright as new. I have two surgeons standing by in the wings, just waiting to come on stage and go in there and fix you up like new."

My mother stared at him. Her eyes narrowed, and in as strong and firm a voice as she could muster, she said these words to him:

"I want you to understand something. This is my body. It is not your body. It is my body. I own it. I will tell you what you may or may not do with my body and my son will enforce it. There will be NO surgery. There will be NO chemotherapy. There will be NOTHING done that will keep me from dying a natural death."

I said to the doctor: "She means it." He stared for a moment at both of us and turned and left the room.

After a long, painful process of decision making, we moved her from intensive care to a nursing home where she could receive 24-hour attention.

As my wife and I were walking down the halls one day looking into rooms where bodies were strapped to beds, bodies that had no idea who and where and what they were, my wife said out loud, to anyone within earshot, "This is a torture chamber."

Once back in Idaho, I was relating this experience to a good friend of mine, a Boise doctor.

His response was: "We in the medical profession can take no pride in what we are doing to those older persons in those conditions. A triumph of medicine? Hardly. Keeping bodies alive cannot be considered a triumph if the mind is gone. The heart of the matter is this: Physicians cannot do it. The politicians and the courts will not do it. THE INDIVIDUAL MUST DO IT."

My doctor friend did not mince words. He said it well. It is a problem that we as a society, collectively, in fear and trembling, are refusing to deal with. And yet it is a problem that we all — every last one of us — are going to have to deal with individually.

In an issue of *New Republic* there was an excellent article by Colorado Governor Richard D. Lamm, entitled *Long Time Dying*. I recommend it to all concerned with this problem. I pass on to you one quote from the article. It was from *Nursing* magazine. A nurse wrote: "We cannot shut our eyes to the fact that resuscitation machinery is very expensive, and if the equipment is not used there is no return on the investment."

Today in these United States, there are hundreds of thousands of persons existing — not living, existing — in continuing, sustained baffled, misery, in pain and anguish, imprisoned in nursing homes and hospitals, isolated, alone, prolonging miserable and painful day after miserable and painful day. I do not think that I overstate the situation when I call it a crime. A crime against humanity.

That "great dane," theologian and philosopher, Soren Kierkegaard asks this question: "What is reflection? Only this. Simply to reflect on these two questions. How did I get into this world and how do I get out of it again? How does it all end for me? What is thoughtlessness? Only this, to muster everything in order to drown out all thought about my own exit."

To Die With Dignity

The subject of euthanasia will become increasingly important for the rest of this century.

Mist clouds my eyes as I remember the last days of my own father, begging the doctors to let him go home and die peacefully in the room he so loved, overlooking the trees and gardens that he had created over the years.

"No," they said, "you must stay here where we can watch you." Maybe brutal is not a strong enough word to describe the situation. And so my father was refused his sacred right to die with integrity, quality and with some dignity left intact in the life of a proud and good man.

I am talking about the right of an individual to determine the quality of his life, and to be able to live and die by that personal determination. I ask you this: Who has made life an imperative, a sentence, an order reserved only for the human animal but apparently denied to all other forms of life?

We talk about human freedom, but if we truly cherish human freedom, it would follow that one, in freedom, can freely choose to terminate his own existence.

Dr. Otis Bowen calls himself a country doctor living in Washington, D.C. He heads the giant Department of Health and Human Services, which includes the Food and Drug Administration.

In a recent interview, he said that his approach to drugs and the dying has been drastically altered as the result of watching his wife go through horribly painful day after painful day dying from bone marrow cancer. Her bones would break when she would try to turn over in bed. He tried to help her turn on one very bad day and broke her collar bones. Nothing was relieving the pain. So the good doctor took the matter in his own hands and gave her marijuana. In his words, "It worked like magic."

In 1981, addressing a major American medical convention, Bowen asked them, "Why can't a dying person have access to *anything they want?*"

A number of years ago, I read of a most remarkable death, that of a 7-year-old boy in Santa Barbara, California. His little frame was shriveled with leukemia. He put on a tape before he died a message of hope that was so articulate it was difficult to remember that he was only 7.

After finishing his taped message, he asked his mother to turn off the support systems, saying to her, "I do not need it anymore." The boy's mother said, "I turned the machines off, at my son's request. He held my hand and gave me a big smile. He then said to me, "It is time mother, good bye," and he died.

He died at home where he wanted to be after deciding all of the details of his own funeral and how he was to be buried. The child was rare. When he was only 4, his mother said, he was studying Eastern religions on his own, without any influence from his parents. California law permits a "living will," but this was the first time the law had been tested due to a child's request.

The question is: How can we all, dying patient, the family, the doctor, nurse, minister, society, the law, the human animal calmly and gracefully accept the mortality of our own condition?

I do believe, with all of my heart, that with total freedom of choice, we have a right to die with dignity as a humane, human being and not as a vegetable in a nursing home or on the third floor of some hospital, extending existence through senseless and cruel days, days that can be classified and labeled as terrorism.

"Nowadays it is difficult to die. We feel that this way we are taking will become more usual and acceptable as the years pass."

> — *Dr. Henry Pitney Van Dusen*
> *and his wife in a note they*
> *left prior to dying*

"Why are so many people more readily appalled by an unnatural form of dying . . . than by an unnatural FORM OF LIVING."

> — *Norman Cousins, Editor,*
> **The Saturday Review**

Clowns of Creationism

The circus that recently played within the walls of state capitols, produced by the clowns of creationism, brought back to my mind the pathetic comedy of the Scopes trial of 1925 in Dayton, Tennessee.

William Jennings Bryan was brought in as the champion of the creationists. Clarence Darrow offered to defend John Scopes, the biology teacher who was being tried for teaching evolution. The following exchange will explain what I mean by "the clowns of creationism." The *New York Times* called it the most unbelievable court scene in Anglo Saxon history.

Darrow: "You have given considerable study to the *Bible*, haven't you Mr. Bryan?"

Bryan: "Yes, I have studied the *Bible* for over 50 years."

D.: "Do you claim that everything in the *Bible* should be literally interpreted?"

B.: "Yes, I believe what the *Bible* says. I believe the *Bible* absolutely."

D.: "Do you believe the story of the flood to be literal?"

B.: "Yes, absolutely."

D.: "When was that flood?"

B.: "I would not attempt to fix the day."

D.: "Well, what do you think?"

B.: "I do not think about things that I do not think about."

D.: "Do you ever think about things that you do think about?"

B.: "Sometimes."

D.: "How long ago do you think the flood was, according to the *Bible?*"

B.: "Two thousand, three hundred and forty eight years, B.C."

D.: "And every living thing not on the ark was destroyed?"

B.: "The fish might have survived. They could swim."

D.: "And you believe that all civilizations, and every living thing, except maybe the fish, was completely wiped out by the flood?"

B.: "Yes."

D.: "Don't you know that there are ancient civilizations thousands of years older than your creation date?"

B.: "No, that is not so, they would not run back beyond the biblical creation."

D.: "You do not have any knowledge of ancient civilization, is that right?"

B.: "I do not know how old they are."

D.: "Do you have any idea how old the Egyptian civilization is Mr. Bryan?"

B.: "No."

D.: "Do you know how old Chinese religion is?"

B.: "No."

D.: "Do you know how old the religion of Zoroaster is?"

B.: "No sir."

D.: "Have you ever tried to find out?"

B.: "No. . . ."

D.: "Do you believe that the sun was literally made on the fourth day?"

B.: "Yes."

D.: "Well, then, according to the story they had an evening and morning, the first three days without the sun."

And on and on it went.

Will Rogers, America's beloved columnist, wrote these serious words in his next syndicated column:

"All the other things that William Bryan has been wrong on didn't do much harm. But, now, when he says he is going to make it (the *Bible*) a political issue, and get it into the Constitution of the United States, he just can't ever do that. He might make Tennessee the side show of America, but he can't make a street carnival of the whole United States."

It was left to H. L. Mencken to send the following paragraph to his home paper, *The Baltimore Evening Sun:*

"William Bryan once had a leg in the White House. Now he is a tinpot pope in the Coca-cola belt and a brother to the forlorn pastors who belabor half-wits in galvanized iron tabernacles behind the railroad yards. His own speeches were grotesque, touching on imbecility."

Now, 60 years after the Scopes trial, the psycho-ceramic (crack-pot) circus played again in the state capitol of Idaho.

Myths of Creation

The diffusion of mythological themes from one culture to another and one religion to another is well known to religious historians. It is obvious with origin or creation mythologies.

Actually, the oldest Biblical accounts of creation are not the myths of *Genesis,* but *Psalm 104.* This psalm was borrowed from the famous "hymn of the Sun" of Akhenaton, Egypt's great monotheistic Pharaoh (1377-1360 B.C.).

As for the creation mythology of *Genesis,* both accounts were borrowed from other religions and both contradict one another. In *Genesis 1,* man is the last of the creation myth. In Chapter 2, man is the first to be created, with all else being created later.

These creation stories are recognized as mythological themes in the religion departments of every major university in this country (as well as the world), and also in the theological seminaries of the majority of mainline Protestant denominations. Only fundamentalist schools refuse to recognize the scholarship of these and related Biblical studies.

The *Interpreters Bible* is a 12-volume series, with contributions from 125 of the most eminent Biblical scholars in the world.

The exegetical commentary on the *Genesis* creation stories is filled with the relationship between these mythologies and those of Babylonian and Persian origin.

For example: "The Babylonian creation myth which echoes throughout the Biblical story must earlier have become a part of Israel's religious heritage."

And again: "The idea of man being created in the image of God is probably dependent on Babylonian mythology," and then following are all the reasons why.

Biblical dictionaries state without hesitation that the "'man made in the image of God' part of the myth is a direct copy of the Babylonian story where Aruru forms a mental image of the God Anu . . ." And Marduk before making man, using his own blood, took counsel with Ea, the high god of wisdom in Babylonian mythology.

As I have said, the diffusion of mythological themes from one religion to another is common knowledge to religious historians. This is as true of the New Testament as of the Old Testament.

The great Heb-Sed festival of ancient Egypt, for example, was celebrated to reaffirm the Pharaoh as divine, or 'God's son.' And in the giant processional that was part of the event, 14 of his ancestors had to precede the Pharaoh in the parade. If 14 were not still living, statues were carried, for 14 had to be the number to reaffirm divinity.

Now, if you read the genealogical table of Jesus in the opening pages of *Matthew,* you find exactly the same mythological formula, of 14 times three. Chapter 2, verse 17 reads: "All the generations from Abraham to David were Fourteen, and from David to the deportation Fourteen, and from the deportation to Babylon to the Christ Fourteen." You have 14 times three. Of course three is the well know triple formula, expressing the numinosity of the "thrice holy" or "holy, holy, holy."

Next, three times 14 equal 42. In Egyptian mythology, you had to appear before Osiris (the god of resurrection who overcame death) and with Osiris had to be 42 of his judges. You had to face them all after you died.

It is fairly obvious that the mythology surrounding Osiris became a part of the Christ mythology that was built up around the figure of the historical Jesus by the early developing church.

The study of mythological diffusion by anthropologists and religious historians is mandatory for anyone wanting to be a serious student of religion, as well as their own Christianity.

For starters, I would suggest reading the three-volume series *The Masks of God* by Joseph Campbell. The volumes include *Oriental Mythology, Primitive Mythology* and *Occidental Mythology.* I also recommend Campbell's *The Hero With a Thousand Faces,* which is a fairly standard university text in religious studies.

A POT-POUR-RI
OF RELIGION

Reincarnation

That brilliant genius, Johann Wolfgang von Goethe, author of *Faust*, wrote "I have lived a thousand times and will be born a thousand times again." He believed in reincarnation.

The *Bible* is loaded with statements supporting earlier existence and reincarnation, and some of the most prominent early church fathers believed in reincarnation. Thousands of the greatest scholars, scientists and thinkers, past and present, have believed in it. They have absolutely rejected the propaganda of orthodox Christian doctrine, which states that there is no such thing.

In A.D. 553, the Second Council of Constantinople said that all who believed in reincarnation would be "cursed." Why?

Suppose you are a bishop with God-like power. If people wake up to the fact that you are not needed to get them into some place called "heaven," and you are coming back again, there goes all of your bishop power right down the tube.

It's obvious that more and more people who are active in Christian churches are coming to believe in reincarnation. In *Adventures in Immortality*, by George Gallup, Jr., Protestants, Roman Catholics and Jews were questioned for a survey published four years ago. "Of all adults polled, 23 percent or nearly one quarter, said they believe in reincarnation," Gallup stated. "Belief in reincarnation rises to 27 percent among those who live in the West. One third, or 30 percent, of those 18 to 24 said they believe in reincarnation."

My own experience during 28 years of serving Presbyterian and Congregational churches suggests that it has been closer to 50 percent. That estimate is based on polls that I have taken, as well as statements made in study groups and social groups.

It is interesting to read writings of early church fathers who firmly believed in preexistence and reincarnation. They include Justin Martyr (A.D. 100-165), who also believed in metempsychosis, which holds that souls come back in other bodies, including animals; St. Clement of Alexandria (A.D. 150-220); Origen (A.D. 185-254); St. Gregory (A.D. 257-332); and St. Jerome (A.D. 340-420).

But, in the Second Council of Constantinople, ecclesiastical curses (or anathemas) were charged against Origen, and anyone else who held this belief. The curses end with this line: "whomsoever there is who thinks thus, or defends these opinions, or presumes to protect them shall be cursed."

Over the years thousands upon thousands of highly intelligent people have laughed at these "curses," and the other garbage coming from that Second Council 1,500 years ago.

Brilliant human beings who have believed in reincarnation include: Pythagoras, Plato, Aristotle, Michelangelo, Nietzsche, Schopenhauer, Thoreau, Walt Whitman, Thomas Huxley, Julian Huxley, Thomas Edison, Albert Schweitzer, Bruno, Sir Francis Bacon, William Shakespeare, John Donne, John Milton, William Blake, Robert Browning, Alfred Lord Tennyson, Charles Dickens, George Bernard Shaw, Rudyard Kipling, H. G. Wells, Richard Wagner, Victor Hugo, Soren Kierkegaard, Dostoevsky, Tolstoy, Boris Pasternak, Benjamin Franklin, Ralph Waldo Emerson, Oliver Wendell Holmes, Robert Frost, Edgar Allan Poe, Mark Twain, Charles Darwin, Charles Lindbergh, Albert Einstein.

Among the giants of American clergy who have believed in reincarnation were the Congregational ministers Edward and Henry Ward Beecher, as well as Episcopalian Bishop Phillip Brooks.

I think you get my thesis: a great many of the intellectual and spiritual giants of civilization have believed, and do believe, in the potential, or the actuality of reincarnation.

To illustrate, the genius Goethe chose these words for his *Song of the Spirits Over the Waters:*

"the soul of man is like to water.
From Heaven it cometh . . .
To Heaven it riseth . . .
And then returneth to earth,
Forever alternating . . ."

Origins of 'Religion'

Hanging on the wall of my study is a remarkable map. It is about 3 feet wide and 6 feet long. It shows the history of religious evolution starting 180,000 years ago and ending at the bottom in 1966. The title is "The History Map of Religion." It is in eight colors, with each representing a flow of mythologies and concepts from one religion to another.

For instance, if you follow the color blue, you can see the mythological diffusion, or continuity, from Zoroastrianism and Mithraism into Christianity. It is quite an educational experience to stand in front of it and study the overall evolution of religions from the third (warm) interglacial period; the Lower Mousterian Culture of Neanderthal man in Europe to the religious picture of the Earth in 1966.

We ask: "Where did it all begin, this impulse, or this behavior, that we call 'religious'." How far back do we go to find the origins of some of our beliefs, like life after death, or the belief in supernatural beings and spirits?

Anthropologists think religious behavior can be traced as far back as the Neanderthal period. Why do they think so?

Because the Neanderthal people buried their dead with great sensitivity and care. Flowers were put into the graves. Artifacts were buried with the dead, with two primary purposes. The artifacts either were to go with you into another life after death, or they were offered as gifts to the gods.

We ask: "What led them to believing in supernatural beings and life after death?"

There are a number of theories. The two that I am the most comfortable with are "fear" and "dreams."

We all know what fear can do, and when you realize that the Neanderthal people could not possibly have had an explanation for lightning and forest fire, earthquake and storm, thunder and gale, what else would they think but that supernatural beings were behind it all and had to be placated, worshipped and feared?

Fear must have played a major part in developing ideas about supernatural beings. Even in our own time, it is fear that drives millions to churches and to their knees.

As for life-after-death beliefs, I like the dream theory better than any. We all know how vivid, alive, real and moving dreams can be.

My father died more than 10 years ago, and yet I have had dreams where he and I were doing things that were so sharp, so clear, that I could not believe it was a dream.

Now, what would you think if you were living in the Neanderthal period, and you knew that you had buried one of your friends, long,

long ago, and yet, last night, in a vivid dream, once again he was alive and he was with you again. But, how could that be, for he died and was buried long ago?

And yet, there he was last night, with you again. Why, he must live still. Your friend is not dead at all. He is alive in some other place that follows death.

From such a beginning, thousands and thousands of years ago, there developed rituals and mythological motifs that have spread from at least the Neanderthal period through Cro Magnon caves and into the Christian churches and cathedrals of 20th century America.

Mark Twain and Religion

Huckleberry Finn is over 100 years old. There were many celebrations, not only of Huck Finn's birthday but Mark Twain's genius.

One of the finest stage shows in America was *Mark Twain Tonight*, with Hal Holbrook. Ernest Hemingway paid his tribute to Mark Twain in these words: "All modern American literature comes from one book by Mark Twain, called *Huckleberry Finn*." T. S. Eliot called it "one of the permanent symbolic figures of fiction." William Dean Howells has called Mark Twain "The Abraham Lincoln of American literature."

The word brilliant may be overused, but surely in the case of Mark Twain it applies. He seems forever contemporary. His linguistic needles are as sharp, his observations on the human race as precise, and his sarcasm and humor as glittering today as they were when he originally placed pen to paper.

I guess that everybody has read *Huckleberry Finn*, but I find few who have read Twain's *Letters From the Earth*, a book that is filled with his observations on something that we call "religion." That book made my summer a few years back.

For several glorious and wondrous weeks I lived in a teepee high on an alpine meadow in the mountains of Montana. After getting my new home in order, I lay down under a mountain sun, bathed by cool afternoon breezes, and started reading Twain on "religion." Perhaps some samples will whet your appetite for more:

"The *Bible* tells about creation. God did it. He did not call it the "universe." That name is modern. His whole attention was upon our world. He constructed it in five days . . . and then? It took him only the one remaining day to make 20 million suns and 80 million planets and 8 billion galaxies. (Twain would have had a field day with today's creationists.)

"Darwin was wrong. Man has certainly, obviously, not ascended from any lower animals. He has, quite obviously, descended from the Higher Animals, the apes and primates, to the lower animal that man now is . . . (stupidly fighting over religious creeds and doctrines . . . man made).

"Now I am going to really put a strain upon you. Man thinks he is the noblest work of God. This is the truth I am telling you. Man really believes that. He even hires preachers to tell him so once a week. And very few even laugh. Man, the special pet, whom God has given mumps, measles, whooping cough, croup, colds, asthma, bronchitis, itch, cancer, cholera, typhus, piles, constipation, warts, pimples, boils, corns, tumors, insanity, jaundice, bunions, abscesses, diseases of every organ in the body, but why continue the list? . . ."

If you do not take yourself, or your religious creeds, too seriously, and if you can take a good sharp look at our human species and laugh at the foolish little games that we play, then you will love *Letters From the Earth*. But if you are religiously thin and tight lipped, out to save the world and judging others through squinted eyes, then *Letters From the Earth* is for you too. Twain may guide you through and out of your labyrinth.

"God's incomprehensible conduct toward the creatures his OMNIPOTENCE had made, whose inadequacies He must know by virtue of that same omnipotence . . . and whom moreover it pleased Him to lead astray . . . is all a part of that mindless babbling that characterizes so much religious 'education'."

— Carl Jung

Language as Symbol

"I know you believe you understand what you think I said, but I'm not sure you realize that what you heard is not what I meant."

That little bit of truth hangs, framed, in my office to remind me constantly of the symbolism of language and that each separate individual will be receiving and interpreting the linguistic symbols differently. How you read or hear word symbols will depend upon your ethnic background, educational background, as well as social, economic, religious, parental and emotional background and experiences.

There are few subjects more important in the study of religion than the study of language. How you perceive the world, the cosmos and yourself, religiously, is directly dependent upon your language and your personal vocabulary.

Some examples: the Hebrew language of the Old Testament has no vowels and no punctuation. It is just miles of consonants; and also 'backwards' in that you read from right to left, rather than from left to right as we do in English, and the beginning is, what would be to us, the back of the book. Now, some translator must fill in both vowels and punctuation. A series of Hebrew consonants can mean any number of different words depending upon what vowels the translator chooses. And what punctuation the translator chooses can change the meaning of a sentence completely.

For instance: "I will lift up mine eyes into the hills, from whence cometh my help" (period). That is the way the King James reads. Since that time scholars have learned that it is not a period at all, but a question mark that should end that statement, as you now have in the Revised Standard translation. That is not any earth-shaking event considering the passage just quoted, but you can see how precarious it becomes to base your entire 'beliefs' or 'salvation' on any one translation, of either the Old or New Testament.

To move on now to the language of the Hopi Indians. Hopi verbs have no tense, no past and no future. How would you like to translate Hebrew into Hopi? You remember that old thing about "it lost something in the translation." Well, let me tell you, it loses *everything* in the translation, if a translation was even possible.

Or, consider the Navajo language. You may remember that the Marine Corps in World War II used Navajo Indians in the South Pacific to talk to each other on the radios to pass on orders and it drove the Japanese crazy. They never could break the code of the Navajo just speaking his own language. One vocal sound in Navajo can mean many different things. It depends upon the pitch of the sound, the inflection and other considerations.

Now, my bottom line as they say, is this: You and I (human beings) do not live in an objective world alone. We are very much at the mercy of our particular language, which has become our medium of expression. Our concept of "reality" and of the "real world" is built upon our language and our individual vocabulary. And this includes our *religious* orientation. No two languages are similar enough to represent the same reality.

I am always left staggered after hearing someone say they know exactly what salvation means after reading that English word in some English biblical translation. In my library are four volumes of Scribners *Dictionary of the Bible.* Each volume is about 4 inches thick. The print is so small I need a magnification glass oftentimes. Under the word salvation, there are *18 pages,* covering all problems that are related to that word, all of the different meanings and ways it was used in Hebrew, in Greek, in the mystery religions and on for 18 pages.

What John Doe does not seem to ever realize is that the way he is interpreting that word symbol "salvation" written in the English language in 1988, could have absolutely no relationship to the original use of that word symbol, say in Hebrew, thousands of years ago when it was first written.

What all of this says is this: Your religious beliefs and how you think of yourself in relation to "God," the universe, your neighbor is totally dependent upon your language and also your own particular vocabulary and understanding of the linguistic symbols that you daily use and with which you think.

I am well aware that after I have written this column there will be as many different responses and interpretations as there are readers. Language shapes our lives and our religious beliefs. Understanding this can help open up the religiously closed mind.

"I know you believe you understand what you think I said, but I'm not sure you realize that what you heard is not what I meant."

About Robert Ingersoll

Several weeks ago at my regular Wednesday noon book review, I presented the life and thought of Robert Ingersoll. About 70 people were present. The majority were university educated and well read, and yet only about 5 percent of the group had heard of Ingersoll.

I have had similar experiences with other groups. What is surprising is that Ingersoll is so little known in our time.

He lived from 1833 to 1899 and was internationally known as the "Great Agnostic," one of the most brilliant thinkers, lawyers, orators, debators and authors of his day — or any day. Twelve volumes of his works are still available and are a collector's treasure. He lectured all over the United States and abroad to standing-room-only audiences.

He spoke on many subjects, but thousands upon thousands turned out to hear him demolish the absurdities of orthodox religious dogmas. He found them repugnant due to the damage they did to the human mind and spirit. He and Thomas Jefferson shared similar views regarding organized religion. And yet, on a deep and profound level he had a sense of the mystery that was breathtaking.

I can tell you that without exception his funeral eulogies are the most beautiful that I have read in the English language. The poet laureate of the universe, Walt Whitman, said that only one man could speak at his funeral, and that man was Robert Ingersoll.

Carl Sandburg said of Ingersoll's eulogy of Whitman, "It was a most precious treasure."

Mark Twain literally idolized Ingersoll. Twain wrote: "I heard four speeches which I can never forget by that splendid soul Bob Ingersoll. It was just the most supreme combination of words ever put together since the world began. His words will sing through my memory always as the divinest that ever enchanted my ears. America will never again see his equal. Of all men, living and dead, I love Ingersoll the most. Except for my daughter, I have not grieved for any death as I have grieved for his."

The greatest man in the Christian pulpit of that day was the Congregational minister Henry Ward Beecher, 200 years ahead of his time, and Ingersoll's closest friend. He and Ingersoll were in complete agreement regarding their views of the *Bible* and Christian dogma and doctrines.

Of Ingersoll, Beecher wrote: "He is the most brilliant speaker in the English tongue. In him, we find the magnificent, glorious flame of genius and honest, free thought."

Some samples of his writings to whet your appetite: "Religion is like a palm tree . . . it grows at the top. The dead leaves are all orthodox, while the new ones are all heretics.

"True religion must be free. Without perfect liberty of mind, there can never be a true religion. Without freedom of thought, the brain is a dungeon, the mind a convict.

"Who can account for the fact, if we are to be saved by faith in Christ, that Matthew forgot it and Luke said nothing about it?"

Ingersoll put down in writing his creed for all of the thousands wanting such a statement from him: "To love justice, to love mercy, to assist the weak, to love the truth, to utter honest words, to love freedom, to love family and friend, to make a joyful home, to love the beautiful in art and nature, to cultivate the mind, to be familiar with the mighty thoughts that genius has expressed, to fill life with generous acts and the warmth of loving words, to destroy prejudice and superstition, to receive new truth with gladness, to cultivate hope and see the dawn beyond the night. This is the religion of reason. This satisfied the heart and the brain."

"Talent develops itself in solitude; character in the stream of life."

— Goethe

More Robert Ingersoll

One of the joyful rewards of writing a column is to receive the delightful letters that arrive in response, with often developing new friendships. After my column on Robert Ingersoll, many wrote, or called, saying the column brought back a bit of nostalgia, because "I remembered how my father (or grandfather, or mother) used to rave about Robert Ingersoll . . . and I had forgotten."

Since my last column was primarily introducing the man to those who had not heard of him, I did not have space to give examples of the gems that flowed from his pen.

Women: "The men who declare that woman is the intellectual inferior of man, do not and cannot, by offering themselves in evidence, substantiate their declaration. Husbands as a rule, do not know a great deal, and it will not do for every wife to depend on the ignorance of her worst half.

"It is the women of today who are the great readers. No woman should have to live with a man whom she abhors. I despise the man that has to be begged for money by his wife. 'Please give me a dollar?' . . . 'What did you do with 50 cents I gave you last Christmas?' he asks."

Government: "I despise the doctrine of state sovereignty. States are political conveniences. Rising above states as the Alps above valleys are the rights of man, the sublime rights of the people . . . Nothing is farther from democracy than the application of the veto power. It should be abolished. . . . I do not believe in being the servant of any political party. I am not the property of any organization, I do not believe in giving a mortgage on yourself or a deed of trust for any purpose. It is better to be free."

Church and state: "Church and state should be absolutely and totally divorced. . . . Presidents and governors should never issue religious proclamations. It is not part of their official duty. It is outside and beyond the horizon of their authority. There is nothing in the Constitution to justify this religious impertinence. . . . Jefferson, when president, refused to issue a 'Thanksgiving proclamation,' on the grounds that the government had no business making religious statements. He was quite right."

Bible: "Any woman who regards the *Bible* as the charter of her rights will always be the slave of man. . . . If a person would follow the teachings of the *Old Testament*, he would be a criminal. If he would strictly follow the teachings of the *New Testament*, he would be insane. . . . Jesus never wrote a solitary word of the gospels and he never told anybody to write a word. . . .

"Was Adam the first man? Who was Cain's wife? Who was the snake? How did he walk? What language did he speak? This turns a church into a nursery and makes a cradle out of each pew, and gives to each member a rattle with which he can amuse what he calls his mind."

Jesus: "Jesus takes his place with other teachers of mankind. He hated oppression; he despised superstition and hypocrisy; he attacked the heartless church of his time; he received the hatred of bigots and priests; he was an infidel in denouncing the orthodox religion as it then existed. . . . What if Jesus was an illegitimate child, I would think no less of him.

"Nothing ever was, nothing ever can be more perfectly idiotic and absurd than the dogma of the trinity. . . . A creed is the ignorant past bullying the enlightened present. . . . A Christian who does not believe in absolute intellectual freedom is a curse to mankind. An agnostic or 'infidel' who does believe in absolute intellectual freedom is a blessing to the world.

"Is life worth living? How I love life, to be alive, to breathe the air, to look at clouds and stars, read poems, listen to good music, hear the voices of my loved ones."

"A human being should live only in harmony with his very own nature . . . and according to his VERY OWN nature. He should live in accordance with the truth about himself."

— *Carl Jung*

"A truly creative person has little power over his own life. He is captive and driven by his creative energies."

— *Carl Jung*

Trust Your Own Experiences

I was invited to speak to the Eastern Idaho Unitarian Fellowship at Idaho Falls. They chose this subject for me: "How to develop your own personal theology and religious philosophy, free from authoritarian direction."

I devoted my lecture time to four steps:

1. Begin by taking a hard, critical look at all so-called religious authorities.

2. Then learn to trust your very own personal experiences and intuition. Thomas Jefferson said this well: "Your own reason is the only oracle given to you by God."

3. Accept the risks that go with taking control of your own life and its direction.

4. Enjoy the joys and freedom that go with such a new orientation.

It is interesting to me that this is exactly the same subject that was requested for my lectures at the University of Alabama Conference Center. I was asked to explore Carl Jung's question: "Why are so many millions willing and eager to turn their lives over to outside authorities?" The more that we depend on outside authorities for direction, the more is our own growth and creative unfoldment arrested.

And yet, how many still yearn for an outside religious authority to pat us on the head and tell us that we have been "good," or to slap our little hands and tell us that we have been "bad," ensuring that we stay forever emotionally stunted and dwarfed spiritually?

One of Buckminister Fuller's most brilliant observations says it all: "All organized religions of the past were developed as beliefs in secondhand information. It will be an entirely new era when man finds himself confronted with direct experience."

There it is: direct experience. In the first chapter of the gospel of Mark, it is written that "Jesus taught as one who had authority, and not as the Scribes." Jesus, an authority? An authority about what?

Jesus is certainly not my authority in science. Any seventh-grader today knows more about the world than did Jesus. Jesus knew nothing about DNA molecules, Vitamin E or splitting atoms. Jesus is certainly not my authority in music, archaeology, anthropology, history, medicine, law, horticulture, agronomy or philosophy.

So, in what way was Jesus an authority about anything? In only one way: He spoke about his personal direct experience with the mystery and the sacred. He trusted his very own, unique, direct experience, rather than the secondhand information of the Scribes and the Judaic law.

It should be the same today for you, for me. It is not to the authoritarian institutions that we look, for they possess only secondhand information. Rather, it is to our own direct experience with the mystery that we call God. Jesus pointed toward a new consciousness in his own time, saying that no one who looks back is fit for the kingdom. You cannot put new wine into old wineskins, he said. That truth is equally valid for our own time.

There is new wine for this new time, this new year. The same spirit that flowed through Jesus still flows, for you, for me. When we experience this, we will never again need anyone to tell us about God in a secondhand way, and we will be contributing toward the development of a new spiritual consciousness even greater than the old wine that was Jesus. Our species and our planet wait.

"Naturally . . . nature has so disposed me."

— Leonardo da Vinci

"I determined from that moment on . . . never again to let anyone push me . . . in any direction . . . not in HARMONY WITH MY OWN NATURE."

— Carl Jung

"All of my clients ask, basically the same thing . . . 'how can I live in harmony with my REAL SELF . . . underneath all of my surface behaviour?'"

— Erich Fromm

"There must come a time in one's life . . . when he finally says . . . 'this is ME . . . and the rest of the world can go to hell' . . ."

— Dostoevsky

Enjoying Your Dinner

"This beef steak is dead . . . the spirit is gone. . . . I'll not eat it."

So said a 96-year-old Huichol shaman (holy man) to the waiter at one of New York City's most exclusive restaurants. Now, you might ask: Who are the Huichols, what did he mean, and what was he doing there? I'm glad you asked.

The Huichol people live in the remotest areas of the Sierra Madre Occidental of Mexico. A friend of mine, the anthropologist Joan Halifax (author of *Shamanic Voice*), completed her doctoral field work with them. Matsuwa, their most revered holy man, became her good friend.

After returning to Columbia University, Joan thought it would be a wonderful gift to fly Matsuwa to New York City and show him the sights. This 96-year-old holy man had never left his native village. His observations, overall, were that New York City was "sick," and the people had lost their souls.

One evening Joan, and friends, took Matsuwa to dine at a fine restaurant. Matsuwa wanted meat, so they ordered the best filet that the house had to offer. When the waiter placed the steak in front of him, Matsuwa picked it up in his hands, smelled it, turned it over and smelled it again. He promptly pronounced to all (through a translator) that "this meat is dead . . . the spirit is gone . . . bad for you. . . . I'll not eat it."

The matre d' still has not recovered. Matsuwa later explained that only fresh vegetables and fresh meat, newly killed, still contain the vital life energy, life spirit, that makes one healthy and strong. (He sired children into his early 90s).

"There is more to food than just passing through your body. There are spirits in food. I was brought up to regard food as something sacred," said John Lame Deer, a holy man of the Oglala Sioux.

In Taoist thought of ancient China, much like Matsuwa, food, while fresh possessed "chi," the "vital energy," "the stuff of life," and when ingested reinforced the "chi" of our own bodies. "What is eaten is sunlight. The breath of life is the clouds, and the blood is the rain that falls on the world." (Ogotemmeli)

Food, as far back as can be traced, has been associated with the spiritual. Rice and milk, barley and wine. Visible food becomes transformed in us into food for immortality. There is only transformation. It is an eating world. Feeding, we are fed. We become what we eat. We must eat food to think, and we live by our thoughts. Remembering that the liver performs more than 500 vital, miraculous functions, I may do a column on the spirituality of the liver, considering that we could not spiritually function without it. Not in this lifetime.

Through sacred food and drink our spirits are nourished. There is a sacred cosmic metabolism, a cosmic transformation.

"I died as a mineral and became a plant. I died as a plant and rose to an animal. I died as an animal and I was man. Why should I fear? When was I less by dying? And once more shall I die as Man to soar with spirits blest," wrote Rumi.

Food, has been a symbol of the divine reality throughout almost all of the major religious traditions. Food, as God, Brahman, Vishnu, Jesus, Horus, Ra.

"I am food. I am the food eater. I am the combining agent. I am the first born, earlier than the gods, the center of immortality. I who am food, have overcome the world." (From the Upanishad)

"When you taste food, if you know who it is that tastes it, then you have known HIM." (Brahman) "Food is the body of the blessed Vishnu." (Hinduism) "I am the divine soul, the divine food, Ra, God." (Egypt)

And 3,000 years *before* Jesus, it was written in Egypt of their divine child, Horus: "Horus is the divine food." From Christianity: "Jesus took bread and give it to his disciples saying, Take, eat, this is my body."

Maybe we have lost something precious. In too many families the evening dinner hour has become a battleground, a forum for argument. How many homes would be blessed by a recovery of the spiritual consideration of the evening dinner hour, with families eating together in an atmosphere of beauty, pleasant conservation, laughter and joy, love and sharing, with body and spirit being fed.

The biblical author of *Ecclesiastes* reminds us: "Go, eat your bread with enjoyment, and drink your wine with a merry heart. Enjoy life with a wife whom you love . . . all the days that you have been under the sun."

About Living Water

My wife and I had a marvelous two and a half weeks in Mexico City and Cancun. It was a vacation that I have long awaited — to see and to study the religious symbols, artifacts and shrines of the Aztec and Mayan people. I am not aware of another museum in the world equal to the National Museum of Anthropology in Mexico City. I am at a loss to find words that could adequately describe it; you must see it to believe it.

The role that water has played in all of the religious mythologies of the world has long fascinated me. The belief that water was the primordial home of man is almost universal. In the symbolism of the great Mayan and Aztec pyramids it is paramount. The zero in the Mayan number system represented the ocean, which is endless in time and space. It was the Mayans who first developed a concept of the zero. The "foundation" of the pyramids was water, symbolizing the first world when all was water. Conch shells decorate the walls of Teotihuacan temples, since they they are symbolic of water.

Water is a living element, a spiritual element, and relates us to the other elements of our globe: earth, air and sunlight. Nearly 75 percent of the surface of the earth is water, and that same percentage applies to the water in our own bodies. Menstrual periods, the ocean tides and ground water within the earth all reflect the course of the moon. Tree sap follows the same cosmic rhythm. Lumbermen floated their logs downstream during the new moon, or they would be beached high and dry under a full moon.

"Water, thou are the source of all things and of all existence," says an Indian Vedic text. The biblical creation mythology, which is only a refinement of the Babylonian creation story, tells of a watery chaos, or a primordial ocean.

Primeval waters, as the origin of all worlds, can be found in almost all creation mythologies. An exegetical study on the book of *Genesis* in my library says it this way: "Here in the Hebrew myth, a divine word as an agent of creation is found, as in Babylonian, Egyptian and Indian mythologies, as well as others. In these myths the word is a magic word, the correct formula, which, being uttered released the power to bring order out of a watery chaos."

Since prehistoric times, water, woman and moon were the trinity of fertility for man and the universe. The spiral was the symbol of water and lunar fertility, with the snail, woman and fish.

In the Aztec religion, a mother would say the following while baptizing her new baby in water: "Take this water, for the goddess of waters Chalchiuhtlatonac is thy mother. May this bath cleanse thee of the sins and blemishes thou has received from thy parents." Then touching the breast and head of the child with water, she would say "receive child, thy mother, the divine goddess of all waters."

The phrase "living water," in a spiritual sense, is almost universal in religious traditions. You may recall, that phrase is put into the mouth of Jesus in the *Gospel of John.* Jesus, using an ancient symbolism, tells the woman at the well that he will give her "living water."

"Living water" was thought to ensure eternal life. Water nourishes life, brings to germination all seeds, is the supreme spiritual magic, as well as medicinal substance on this planet. I have often thought that you and I, Homo sapiens, could totally disappear from the earth and it would make no difference to the life and survival of our delicate planet. (It may survive longer without us.)

But if water were removed from our fragile earth, it would die. No plants, no animals. It would very shortly resemble the surface of the moon. Perhaps, after all, it is not us, but water that is the most sacred and spiritual element on this planet and the most dear to God. Without water there would be only desolation. "Water, thou art the source of all existence."

Art, Cities and the Sacred

My thoughts today have turned toward McCall's great Winter Carnival.

It is the new feature though, The Idaho Snow Sculpting Championship, that has captured my interest and imagination. This is a genuine and authentic art form that deserves our attention.

It is our hope that, in 1990 our Centennial year, we will host the Northwest Regional Snow Sculpting Competition. That would include the states of Washingon, Oregon, California, Nevada, Montana, Wyoming and Colorado.

Now, you may be asking, what has this to do with religion? The answer, historically, is everything.

Cities and towns, with their art and religion, were one and inseparable. Cities were identified by their art. The earliest cities began as tribal shrine centers. An example is the city of Catal Huyuk, going back to 6,000 BC in south central Turkey.

The city, the shrines and its art were inseparable and perceived as one. Shrine centers were located at what was believed to be the axis of the universe, the one place where the earth and the gods connected. Murals were painted freehand on walls by artists.

The colors were strong and vivid. Every third building in the downtown area was a shrine where the most elaborate art-work has been found, all with religious overtones. Cities were "holy" in the true sense of the word, and it was magnificent art that contributed to that "holiness," or the "whole-ness" of both the city and the people.

Cities and towns are places where human beings confront the implications of their humanity and what it means to be truly human, and it was through art forms that the degree of their humanity was revealed. A major factor in pulling a community together with a renewed sense of identification and enrichment is public art.

This is happening in McCall through the new art form of snow sculpting, unique to a mountain resort town known for winter sports and activities. It is no exaggeration to say that there is a sense in which all good art has religious overtones in that it has demanded the best of the human potential for creativity, and has brought to the surface the beauty of aesthetic sensibilities.

The Renaissance, at its best, took seriously the sacredness of the human being and the contribution of great art, music and literature (the humanities) to human and cultural enrichment. The value of public art is that it provided, and still provides, a central expression and focus. It can become the symbol and trademark, even the logo, of a community.

All great art, even good art, can be called "religious" in that it reflects the values of humankind. When placed outside on the plazas and sidewalks of towns and cities it becomes a source of pride, identification and mirrors the spirit and heart of a community.

Lewis Mumford, the social philosoher of Stanford University, said all of this very well: "A community whose life is not irrigated by art, religion and philosophy, day upon day, is a community that exists only half alive. The fundamental values of a true community are to be found in poetry, art, the free use of the imagination, the pursuit of non-utilitarian activities, the production of non-profitmaking goods, the enjoyment of non-consumable wealth . . . here are the sustaining values of a living culture."

Rollie Campbell and the Circle C Ranch

Lush Meadows Valley in Central Idaho, on an early August morning, is surely as beautiful as anyplace else in the entire world. Dew sparkled in new light. The sky was cloudless, reflecting a shade of blue that can only be found at these altitudes in fresh summer dawns.

We were riding toward the distant mountains. White-face cattle were moving to let us pass. Riding beside me on a spirited sorrel was Rollie Campbell, the president and part owner of the once great Circle C ranch of central Idaho.

Riding straight in the saddle, silver hair flowing, it was just impossible to believe that he is approaching his 90th birthday.

How grateful I was that he had invited me to herd cattle with him on this glorious August day. The winds drifting across that meadow carried good smells of cattle and horses and brought to my mind, once again, the joys of childhood summers spent on my grandparents' little West Texas ranch.

But West Texas, love it as I did, does not have the beauty of Meadows Valley. The lush grassland jealously guarded by mountain peaks pushing upward and creating the most magnificent cathedral that God ever made.

It has been said that "they don't make 'em like they used to." Maybe it is so, I thought, as Rollie told me the story of his boyhood.

Rollie's father, Charles, and neighbors went to a great deal of effort and expense to get a school started in that valley. One inviting spring day Rollie and a few friends gave in to the desire to play hooky. The spot they chose for their little picnic was within eyesight of a trail that Rollie's father seldom rode. This day — of all days — he rode by and saw the boys. But he just rode right on.

It was very quiet that evening around the dinner table. Rollie was just about to graduate from the 8th grade. The silence was finally broken when his father announced that Rollie would take the entire 8th grade over next year. Perhaps that would impress upon him the value of an education and the sacrifice that parents had to make for the school and a teacher.

I asked: "Rollie, how do you feel now about that decision your father made?" Without a moment's thought, he answered, "It was right. I should not have played hooky. It taught me something of value."

Today Rollie and his lovely wife, Alma, live graciously and well and are having a marvelous time with this thing called life. They divide their time between the ranch, a lakeside home in McCall and a Boise condominium for the winter months. They make the best Bloody

Marys in Central Idaho and can still dance until the band stops playing.

But it's what he and Alma represent that means so much, to so many, that has long been forgotten by a segment of our society. As Rollie put it: "It is our responsibility to do all that we can to preserve our heritage, the freedom of the individual, the right to be resourceful, self-reliant and independent." He sees the regimentation that is taking place in society today as deplorable.

Riding beside this man, in his own sacred cathedral that he has known for 90 years, I could only think of the moving words from the book of *Job:*

"You shall be in league with the stones of the field, and the beasts of the field shall be at peace with you. You shall know that your tent is safe and that your descendants shall be many and your off-spring as the grass of the earth. And you shall come to the end in ripe old age, as a shock of grain comes to maturity in its season . . . Lo, it is true."

"Either all of nature is a pure revelation of God . . . or there is no revelation."

— William Temple

"Books and men lie. Nature does not lie."

— Thomas Paine

"Nature is the living . . . visible God."

— Goethe

"Wonder . . . astonishment at something awesomely mysterious . . . to marvel."

— Webster's Dictionary

Frank Waters,
Man of the Earth and the Spirit

Frank Waters was nominated in 1987 for the Nobel prize in literature. My heart overflowed with joy as I read that announcement.

This 81-year-old spiritual genius has been one of my role models for more years than I can remember. As a student, scholar and practitioner of the spirituality and cosmology of the Native American Indian he has no peers. The Frank Waters bibliography of fiction, non-fiction, biography and short fiction is staggering in its anthropological and religious dimensions. It is not too much to say that he is one of the true Renaissance men of this century.

Many years ago he settled into his little adobe home in Arroyo Seco outside of Taos, N.M. It has been from that spiritual grounding, that piece of sacred earth, that he has roamed outward from the Maya of the Yucatan to the three mesas of the Hopi to become one of the pre-eminent Indian mythologists of our time.

How did he choose Arroyo Seco as his home? I will let him tell you from his Mountain Dialogues:

"How did I happen to choose this slope of the Sangre de Cristo Mountains for my home? It is 8,000 feet high. The rutted dirt road is almost impassable several months of the year, deep in snow during the winter, and in sticky adobe all spring. My house was a deserted adobe whose roof was falling in and whose foundations needed bolstering. Something about it claimed me. Every place on earth bespeaks its own rhythm of life. Every locality has its own spirit. There is no accounting for the mysterious magnetism that draws and holds us to that one locality we know as our heart's home, whose karmic propensities or simple vibratory quality may coincide with our own. Living here for so long, I still do not have a phonograph, a recording machine or a TV set. Not until only a few years ago did I put in a telephone."

I referred to Frank Waters as a spiritual genius. How does he treat the opening hours, the first light, of each new day? From his exquisite chapter on "Silence" are these opening words: "It is my habit to observe a time of meditation stillness each morning when the sun first tips the rimrock of the mountain range behind my adobe. The place is always the same. A rise in the waist high sagebrush, flanked by a clump of huge gnarled junipers. I did not choose this spot. It simply drew me years ago by some curious magnetism, until I have worn a barely discernible trail to it through sage and chamisa, around clumps of pinion and cedar, and across dry arroyos. Here I sniff the early morning breeze like an old coyote, to assure myself I am in the center flow of its invisible, magnetic currents. To the sun, and to the two oppositely polarized peaks, El Cuchillo and the Sacred Mountain, I offer my morning prayers . . . and then I give myself to . . . silence."

I can assure you that you will not leave any of the writings of Frank Waters without having your spiritual cup filled to overflowing. I would suggest the autobiographical *Mountain Dialogues* and the classic novels *The Man Who Killed the Deer* and *People of the Valley.*

For definitive works in mythology and religion read: *Masked Gods: Navajo and Pueblo Ceremonialism* and *Pumpkin Seed Point: Being within the Hopi.*

Frank Waters was the first white man to receive the revelations of the Hopi's historical and religious world view. The 32 Hopi elders told him the meaning of their religious rituals during the three years that he lived with them. *The Book of Hopi* is the finest work, known to me, about Hopi history and mythology. If your interest is in the Meso-american cultures, you will not be able to put down his *Mexico Mystique, The Coming Sixth World of Consciousness.*

You will find that this man is of the earth, the sacred land of which he is so much a part. His words are like the land, solid, significant, of great substance, never flashy, noisy, superficial or artificial as is so much contemporary literature.

Frank Waters well deserves the Nobel Prize in literature as he celebrates his 81st golden year. I commend him to you.

Lazy People and the 'Common Man'

The parable of the talents, or the use of capabilities, has long been one of my favorites. *(Matthew 25:14-30)*

It is a hard teaching, the story of three men, one given five talents, another two and another only one. Today, instead of using "men," we would say that the story is of three different "persons" and rightly so.

The five-talent person, as well as the two-talent person, used well what they had been given. They developed their potential to the fullest. They were praised for it.

But the one-talent person did nothing with what he had been given. Therefore it was taken from him and given to the person with five talents, who had already, creatively, doubled his talents to five more.

The story is told primarily to highlight the laziness and irresponsibility of the person given only the one talent, who no doubt spent the majority of his time finding excuses for not doing more with his talent.

He was content and lethargic in his failure and lack of development, the typical digit in a mass. He is the common person who chooses to remain common, leaving his or her potential as untouched and undeveloped as if he never had been given even one talent.

One of the most insulting cults that exists in our society today is the religion that worships the "common man." You hear people say, "Oh, they are just good ol' common people, you will like them."

It has been said that "God must love the common person because He made so many of them." Hardly! God did not make them. They made themselves common by hiding their talent and leaving their potential untouched.

"Assuming a normal birth," wrote Buckminster Fuller, "every child at birth is a potential genius."

What greater insult than to be known as a common person? To say a person is common is to say that he is average or mediocre; it is to be classified as one who cannot compete with the best. What a tragic distinction.

The word common in *Webster's Unabridged Dictionary* is defined as "crude . . . without distinction, second rate, inferior, unrefined, cheap, trite, below normal, inelegant."

Can you imagine any greater insult? What a contradiction we have. If you need surgery requiring great skill, you certainly do not want a common doctor. You will pay all you have for the best surgeon in the country.

If your life is to be defended in court, you will avoid like the plague a common lawyer and seek the best lawyer you can afford.

So, where in the world does this insane and absurd praise of common come from?

Before he died, Ernest Hemingway called this "the millenium of the untalented." He said, "Our society is saturated with actors who cannot act, singers who cannot sing, writers who cannot write, teachers who cannot teach, speakers who cannot speak." And we pay them fortunes for their mediocrity.

Our schools are crying for uncommon teachers who are excellent, outstanding and distinguished. Our communities are in desperate need of such people. Our nation and our world cries for men and women who are uncommon, excellent, trained, talented, competent, distinguished and knowledgeable.

How do we take our beautiful one talent and develop it, use it, to make a significant contribution?

An early Greek poet gave us the answer: "Before the gates of excellence, the high gods have placed sweat."

Are Women Human?

"ARE WOMEN HUMAN?" Do you think I joke? In the year 584 A.D., there was held the COUNCIL OF MACON in Lyons, France. Forty-three Catholic bishops and twenty men representing other bishops met to engage in a serious debate on this subject: *Are Women Human?* The vote was finally called for and the results were as follows: Thirty-two voted yes. Thirty-one voted no. Women were declared human by the Roman Catholic 'Christian' church by ONE vote. During the month of March we are celebrating, nationally, Women's History. The history of women in the Christian church, up until this present day, is a history of half-witted, ignorant and warped men who have acted as if they had frontal lobotomies. Listen to these church 'fathers' as we loosely call them.

Tertullian, called the founder of Western theology: "Woman is a temple built over a sewer, the gateway to the devil. Women are the gate of hell." *St. Clement of Alexandria*, in 96 A.D. wrote: "Every woman should be overwhelmed with shame at the thought that she is a woman." *St. John Chrysostom*, 345-407 A.D.: "Among all savage beasts, none is so bestial as woman." *St. Augustine:* 345-430 A.D. "Any woman who does not give birth to as many children as she is capable of, is guilty of murder." (The pro-lifers must love him.) *Martin Luther*, the leader of the Protestant reformation: "Women should stay at home, sit still, keep house and bear children. If a woman grows weary and dies from child-bearing, it does not matter. Let her die bearing children, that is all she is here for." *John Wesley* of Methodist fame, in a letter to his wife: "Wife, be content to be insignificant. Of what loss would it be to God or man had you never been born." *John Knox*, of Presbyterian fame: "Woman was made to serve and obey man."

Now, you may ask, where did they get these sick opinions? Why, where else but from the *Bible*, that book that some people still refer to as God's, without error, word. Christian denominations today still practice these insane cruelties. They never give a thought to Thomas Jefferson's statement that these 'sacred scriptures' are the writings of 'ignorant and bigoted men.'

The Old Testament is so loaded with outrageous abuses regarding women that this short space precludes documentation. Examples from the New Testament: *Corinthians:* 14 states that wives should regard their husbands as they regard God. *Corinthians:* 11 "MAN is the image and glory of God, but woman is the glory of man. Women were created FOR men." (I am sure that *Playboy, Penthouse* and *Hustler* magazines would agree with that view by St. Paul, that neurotic misogynist.)

If you think that we are talking about ignorance in an archaic age, listen to the Rev. Charles Shedd, Presbyterian minister, writing this advice TODAY to his son in a little book called *Letters on How To Treat a Woman.* "Women are simple souls who like simple things. Our family airedale will come clear across the yard just for one pat on the head. Wives are like that, son. She will come across the house, across the room, across almost anything to give you love, if you will just keep patting her on the head." This Presbyterian minister had one of the largest churches in Houston, Texas. Wives and family dogs . . . just give them pats.

If you read *The Crone* by Barbara Walker, published by Harper and Row, you will not be able to get through Chapter 6 on what Christian men have done to women (so-called witches) without a box of Kleenex, assuming you are a normally sensitive person. Christian men executed over 9 million women, in the most horrible and brutal torture known to the imagination. This took place before and after the year 1484 A.D. It is without precedent in history, except for perhaps the Nazi holocaust. Do you not agree that it is simply beyond human comprehension that today, in 1988, this degradation of women still persists in many Christian denominations, with their male-run church, their male ministers, and their male husbands keeping them in 'their place.' It is one of the great crimes of human history.

THE HOLIDAY SEASONS

New Year's Resolutions

In this New Year season, we are thinking of resolutions, changes we are going to make in our lives.

I can tell you that at least 100 times, and maybe far more, over the past 30 years someone, male and female, has made the following remark to me, both in counseling and in private conversation. They will say: "Oh well, he will never change . . . she won't change . . . I have just got to realize that's the way they are, and the way they're going to be." And then sometimes they will add, "Maybe they can't change. Oh well, you can't change human nature, I guess."

It seems to me that this is the final cop-out: "I can't help myself. I can't change . . . you must take me like I am." There are even popular books that say, "I'm Not Much, But I'm ALL I've Got."

My thesis is that we all need to make some changes somewhere in our lives. We can change if we so desire. Human *nature* can be changed if we feel the need to change it or have the desire, the interest, or the motivation.

I looked up nature in the dictionary. It is defined as an "inherent character or trait." I then looked up inherent, which is "the character of something belonging by *settled habit*." "Settled habit" . . . I was hoping that was what I would find. And so . . . human nature could be defined as our settled habits . . . and habits can be changed and broken, if we so desire.

I think human nature can be changed. And why do I think that? Because it seems obvious to me that it HAS changed. Unless I have missed something somewhere in my thinking. It is through change that we have become what we are now, whatever that is. Why would anyone think that the process is terminated, finalized and completed?

To be human is to be willing to choose and to make choices that affect changes for the better.

There was a "nature" once. What has become of the nature of that primate from which we sprang in the dim African corner with its chewed fish bones . . . and giant ice age pigs? It has changed. Man, since the beginning, seems to be awaiting the arrival of a nature of which he does not know.

Do you realize that at any time in the past million years, if you had looked at this upright, ground-dwelling species and said, "This, finally, is man," you would have been wrong? Had you gazed at Olduvai Gorge man and said, "Ah yes, there now . . . this is man," you would have been wrong. For that creature was not man, but only an upright creature in a moment of time, in the unfolding process of change. And it did not yet appear what it would become.

If you gazed at Java Man and said, "Ah, now . . . now, yes, THIS is man," you would have been wrong.

Had you seen Neanderthal Man and said, "Yes, now, this is man," you would have been wrong.

Had you finally seen Cro Magnon Man and said, "At last, this is man . . ." you would have been wrong.

And now, on this day, when you look at the species of Homo sapiens and you say, "Finally, at last THIS is man," you are oh, so wrong!

For there is always an invisible doorway ahead which, always in a continual process of change and unfoldment, takes us beyond the nature that we know.

What a magnificent opportunity . . . what a grand drama we are a part of . . . to be able to make choices that enable us to transcend genetic and environmental influences, and thus to enter into the continuing process of creation.

The Super Bowl
and Henotheism

SUPER BOWL: Henotheism in 20th century America. Isn't that a great word? We have all heard of polytheism, monotheism, atheism, pantheism, but henotheism, maybe that is a new one for you.

In the study of religions, we are constantly confronted with henotheism. The *Bible* is saturated with it. What it means is this: the worship of your God without denying the existence, sacredness and validity of other gods. A culture, city or state might have their own pantheon (the gods of a people) and sacred symbols that have meaning and significance for them, but they accept the fact that different cultures have other gods that are equally valid and sacred.

Two examples: Each city along the Nile in Egypt had its own pantheon and sacred symbols but they did not deny the validity of the other cities' pantheons. In the Old Testament is the lovely story of Ruth and Naomi. Ruth said to her: "Where you go I will go; and where you lodge I will lodge; your people shall be my people and *your God shall be my God.*" When you changed countries you changed gods. Ruth was saying that she would accept Naomi's god, Chemosh, the God of Moab.

Now, what I am leading up to is this: We, today, in the United States are impregnated with henotheism. What brought this to my mind was an announcement from the Vatican in Rome several years ago. I heard it on my car radio. It left me in such a state of shock that I almost ran a red light, hit two cars and let my pipe fall out of my mouth.

The announcer informed us that the new pope in Rome was going to reschedule the time of his installation out of deference to the Super Bowl football game in the United States (for television considerations). Can you imagine the Super Bowl people rescheduling for the pope? I thought 'thank God, we have finally, at last, got our values and prioroties in the proper and most realistic order.'

I thought of henotheism and sacred symbols. Our athletic teams and the television are our sacred symbols and we have a new henotheism for 20th century America. Each city has its own pantheon (its assemblage of gods) and it worships those, while at the same time accepting the sacredness and validity of all the other cities' sacred symbols and gods.

In Seattle's pantheon are the gods — Seahawks, Sonics, Sounders and Slew. (I don't think the Mariners have made it yet.) The Lions are the chief god in Detroit's pantheon. In Los Angeles, the Raiders. Miami has her Dolphins, and then there is Denver, Kansas City, New York City, St. Louis, Philadelphia, Tampa and on and on and on across all of the great cities of America.

Millions of people worship their gods and they lay millions and millions of dollars on the altar to promote and sustain their pantheon. Remember the old-fashioned places of worship called churches where people dropped a dollar bill in the collection plate on a Sunday morning and often complained that one hour was too long to sit?

Well, that has finally been replaced by the real public worship on Sundays where people will sit for hours in a freezing rain (not all athletic cathedrals have domes), pay 20 bucks for the privilege, yell their lungs out with joy and gratitude and offer thanksgiving.

Oh . . . how often have I wondered: what could happen if all of that massed energy, that time, that commitment, added to those millions and millions of dollars were to be harnessed and applied in some creative and constructive manner to relieve some of the ills of this nation. What a naive dreamer I am. I mean really!

Well, tomorrow the gods who won the cosmic battle finally meet. They collide at Palo Alto, California, to decide who has the greatest and most virile pantheon in all the nation.

Super Bowl XIX . . . Hallelujah! . . . Joyful, Joyful, we adore thee Miami and San Francisco. . . .

Oh yes . . . as you have already guessed. I, too, will be glued to the altar tube to see whose gods are the most powerful and most deserving of worship.

Easter Mythology

The image of a god, buried in a tomb, being withdrawn and said to live again, is thousands of years older than the Jesus stories.

Of all the resurrected savior gods that were worshipped before — and at the beginning of the Christian story — none contributed so much to the mythology developing around Jesus as the Egyptian, Osiris. Osiris was called "Lord of Lords," "King of Kings" and "God of Gods." He was called "the good shepherd," "the resurrection and the life," the god who made "men and women to be born again." He was the Egyptians' "god man" who suffered, died, rose again and lived eternally in heaven.

The Egyptians thought that by believing in Osiris and participating in various rituals they would share eternal life with Osiris. Egyptian scripture says: "As truly as Osiris lives, so truly shall his followers live."

The coming of Osiris was announced by Three Wise Men. His flesh was eaten in the form of communion cakes of wheat. And finally, Egyptians came to believe that only through Osiris could one obtain eternal life.

The much loved 23rd Psalm of the Bible is a modified version of an Egyptian text appealing to Osiris, "the good shepherd," to lead the dead to the "green pastures, and still waters," to "restore the soul" to the body and to give protection in "the valley of the shadow of death."

A number of years ago, there was an outstanding television series of 13 shows called "The Long Search," which documented human religious experience. It was produced for the BBC and shown later in the United States on educational channels.

The section on the ancient Near East was written by Dr. Grace Cairns, who holds a doctorate in religion from the University of Chicago. She wrote: "Because Osiris was human as well as divine, his resurrection signified that every righteous person could likewise rise from the dead and have eternal life if he observed the proper procedures."

She went on to write of the continuity between Osiris and the mythology that accumulated around Jesus. Like the followers of Osiris, the followers of Jesus made him a part of themselves by eating him symbolically so as to participate in his resurrection.

The Bible says: "He that eateth my flesh, and drinketh my blood, dwelleth in me and I in him." (John 6:56).

Gods of that period who were eaten in the form of bread included Adonis and Dionysus, among many others. Other resurrected gods of that period, before Jesus, were Attis and Mithra. Like Jesus, Attis was sacrificed at the spring equinox, rose again from the dead on the third day and ascended to heaven. Like Mithra and the other solar gods, he celebrated his birthday nine months later at the winter solstice.

We are all going to have a joyful time, hiding and looking for Easter eggs with the children. The Easter bunny goes back centuries before Christianity. He was the Moon Hare and sacred to the goddess in many religions.

I like knowing how our rituals fit into the larger picture of our human family. Knowing the origin of our celebrations enriches their dimensions and places us — and our time — within a historical perspective, religiously.

Once again, it relates us to "time past and time future . . . where past and future are gathered . . . pointing to one end . . . which is always present." (T.S. Eliot).

"Easter was the name of the Spring Goddess and was celebrated hundreds of years before Christianity. Originally, Easter was the goddess of the dawn."

— Webster's Unabridged Dictionary

"O Divine Dawn! Enrich and lengthen our lives, O Goddess full of grace! Grant us fulfillment in abundance. O Daughter of Heaven, Dawn of noble birth."

— Hymn to the Dawn
(3000 B.C. Rig-Veda; Hinduism)

Easter and
Life After Death

The distinguished Lutheran Dr. Paul Scherer, was professor of homiletics at Union Theological Seminary, New York City, and also at Princeton University, in the 1960s.

His radio sermons were heard by thousands. His books on preaching still are studied. He once made the observation that the typical Easter story (as heard in the average pulpit) left him with exactly the same feeling as if he had just been fed a 5-pound box of sweet chocolates all at one sitting.

He wrote: "It is not the function of Easter to underscore the notion that we are immortal. The preacher with his platitudes . . . overloads religion."

I know what he was saying. Many seem to think that belief in life after death or resurrection originated with Jesus and was a brand new phenomenon preached by the early Christians. That may sound ludicrous to you, but I run into people who think that, and who also think that is the Easter message and what Easter is all about. It can all get very mushy, syrupy, sticky and sugary, as a "five-pound box of sweet chocolates."

Easter sermons are usually terribly overpreached, with the minister trying to give you a dozen "proofs" about Jesus "rising;" how he did it, where he went and who he is with, and what is going to happen to you as a result of all of that activity. Well, in our more rational moments there are a few other considerations.

Man has believed in life after death for at least 120,000 years, and possibly longer. Death has no finality for any primal peoples. All of them believed that there was a transition from this earthly life to another form of existence following death. In prehistoric times, Neanderthal man deliberately buried his deceased with artifacts and flowers.

In Palestine, 15,000 years before Jesus, a Mesolithic culture buried the dead in extravagant ceremonies, with the bodies heavily ornamented and with many grave goods to be carried over into the next life after resurrection.

In Biblical times, many of the Hebrew people already believed in life after death hundreds of years before Jesus. The Pharisees believed in resurrection long before either the birth or death of Jesus (though the Sadducees did not believe it).

Paul, being a Pharisee, believed in resurrection before the death of Jesus, so saying in his First Letter to the Corinthians, Chapter 15: "If there is no resurrection of the dead, then Christ has not been raised either. If the dead are not raised, then Jesus has not been raised." In other words, as is noted in many exegetical studies, Paul's thoughts about Jesus and resurrection were based on an *already pre-existing belief in resurrection.*

So, there was no point in Jesus's being killed just so he could "prove" some kind of resurrection. He would have been wasting his time. People had *already* believed all of that, firmly and convincingly, including Paul and the Pharisees, for more than 120,000 years.

Martha said to Jesus (before his death) about Lazarus: "I know that he shall rise again in the resurrection."

H. G. Wells once made the observation that "an eternity of H. G. Wells would be intolerable." Even so, the anthropologist Sir James Frazer in *The Golden Bough* wrote: "Of all the many forms which religion has assumed, none has exerted so deep and far reaching an influence on human life as the belief in immortality."

Easter is not concerned with personal survival. Nor with the myriad of imaginative speculations as to what happens while our bodies are decomposing.

The symbolism of Easter rather affirms the power of the living God to transform human life, now, today!

"The hour *now* is (present tense) when the dead that hear shall live. And again, in John: "We know that we have passed (now) out of death into life, because we love. He who does not love remains in death." It is an all satisfying present experience of the love of God. It is eternal life in the midst of time. It is an immediate experience. It is an insight which makes all things new.

I do not think that intelligent, sensitive people want to be fed "a 5-pound box of sweet chocolates all in one sitting" Easter Sunday. I think, perhaps, that many of them would prefer a resurrection of the richness of one word . . . faith.

Faith says: Perceive the wonder that is here today . . . now . . . experience the holy dimensions of existence . . . sense . . . that life is not as dust in the wind . . .

but that, somehow . . . in some way . . .

beyond our feeble comprehension . . .

we are related to something that is ultimate . . .

something that is eternal.

July the Fourth
and Freedom

There is no question in my mind that the 4th of July is the most important holiday that we celebrate in this nation. All of the other national holidays pale by comparison.

Freedom . . . Liberty . . . Equality . . . Justice. . . . "We hold these truths to be self-evident" . . .

The brilliance and genius of our Founding Fathers is beyond imagination. Will we ever again see men, or women, of their stature in this country? Thomas Jefferson: "I have sworn upon the altar of God eternal hostility against every form of tyranny over the mind of man" (political AND religious).

Thomas Paine: "Those who expect to reap the blessings of freedom must, like men, undergo the fatigue of supporting it."

Benjamin Franklin: "Those who would give up essential freedom to purchase a little temporary safety . . . deserve neither liberty or safety."

To read these men makes your blood run faster. You shiver with admiration. We struggled against dictators, tyrants, bigots, dogmatists, the forces of slavery and evil, against those who would shackle and close the mind to free thought and expression.

But we have endured, at the cost of much pain and blood. We have seen one fanatical group after another attempt to kill this ideal that is America. The words liberty, freedom, mean nothing to them.

They wave the flag, big deal, and then deny all that the flag is symbolic of. How ironic, if we should lose all of our hard-won freedoms, not to Russians or terrorists but to right-wing fundamentalists, so-called "Christians," spewing out slogans and cliches.

Several years ago, the Academic Dean of Stanford University wrote these words in their University magazine: "The Christian Right is potentially much more dangerous to our nation than the Communist Party ever has been. This group presents the gravest crisis of this century for the next two decades, because of their wedding of religious slogans with their politics. They are infringing upon a precious right, that each of us inherited from those learned men of the 18th century who expressly separated church and state in these United States of America."

Former Secretary of Education, Terrel Bell, wrote that our textbooks today are being so DUMBED DOWN (by the Christian fundamentalists) that nothing resembling education is taking place in thousands of schools across this country. He wrote that "science texts have degenerated into pablum."

On September 17, 1787, the Constitution of the United States guaranteed us our freedoms, if we, as a free people, assume responsibility for them. This document is the heart of representative democracy.

On the 4th of July weekend, please do forget cold beer and firecrackers for a few moments, and remember some words written by Stephen Vincent Benet. Memorize them. Read them to your children, neighbors and friends. And . . . read them . . . over and over and over again:

"There are certain words . . . Our own and others we're used to . . . words we've used . . . heard . . . had to recite. Forgotten. Rubbed shiny in the pocket, left home for keepsakes . . . inherited . . . stuck away in the back drawer . . . in the locked trunk . . . at the back of the quiet mind.

Liberty . . . Equality . . . Freedom . . . To none will we sell, refuse or deny . . . right or justice. We hold these truths to be self-evident. . . . I am merely saying . . . what if these words pass? What if they pass . . . and are gone . . . and are no more? It took long to buy these words. It took a long time to buy them . . . and much, much pain. . . ."

Thanksgiving Thoughts

My mind is filled with thoughts of Thanksgiving. Thursday is the day we set aside to remember blessings that have enriched our days and graced our lives.

My fingers slide back off the typewriter. I sit back in my chair and let my eyes once again caress the walls of my study, feeling their energy feeding my spirit. The book-lined walls, how I love them.

My heart pours out a very special thanksgiving to all of the great and magnificent spirits whose thoughts and words fill those shelves and offer a feast, waiting only for my mind and soul to partake.

Goethe is there, with Albert Schweitzer and Meister Eckhart, the German theologian. There is Jung, Russell and Whitehead, Loren Eiseley and Suzuki, the Zen master, with Thomas Jefferson and James Madison. There is Learned Hand and Oliver Wendell Holmes, with e. e. cummings, Robert Frost and hundreds more, waiting to once again fill my spirit with food that it timeless.

I think how thankful I will be on Thursday, as well as every other day of the year, for the feast that is offered by the lives and thoughts of great, splendid and radiant human spirits. How much we owe them.

Albert Schweitzer used these words in expressing this thanksgiving: "Sometimes our light goes out but is blown again into flame by an encounter with another human being. Each of us owes the deepest thanks to those who have rekindled this inner light."

And again: "Then a savior appeared to me in the person of my new professor. In the course of the first few days I saw clearly through the mist of my dreaminess . . ." Schweitzer goes on to explain the lasting influence of his outstanding professor.

The radiant aura of Joseph Campbell is illuminating my study this morning. It was a simple announcement in the newspaper: "Joseph Campbell died yesterday in Hawaii at the age of 83." The paper went on to document his international prestige as a historian of religions and mythology.

I stared at the announcement, flooded with memories: studying with him . . . his brilliant mind . . . walks with just the two of us, in the pristine air of a Montana ranch . . .

Then I remembered one very special morning, walking under golden Aspen and hearing him say, "Bill, just keep pointing people toward the Mystery . . . toward the source and the holy . . . just keep pointing them . . . toward the Mystery."

Images of his beautiful wife, Jean, came back to me. She was one of the great dancers with Martha Graham in her younger days and yet, still in her late 70s, was more graceful and lovely than most women much younger.

Later that morning with an almost-absent mind, I started through a cardboard box of letters that had arrived over the years, with "love from Joe and Jean."

A few years ago, the *New York Times Magazine* ran a special interview with Campbell in an Easter edition, referring to him as "the preeminent scholar in the world in mythology and the history of religions."

Bill Moyer has said that his interviews with Campbell were the highlights of his long career on radio and television.

I look back on my studies with Joseph Campbell as one of the great turning points of my life. Never have I learned so much from any other person as I did from that giant scholar, that sensitive and warm human being.

In the words of Schweitzer: "My life was blown again into flame by this encounter with another human being."

I will be saying thank you to the eternal Mystery for the opportunity to know this man, along with all the other glorious spirits that fill the shelves of my study, on this Thanksgiving day.

On Thursday, pause for a moment from the turkey and dressing to think back over your life. Think back to those people who came into your life — those human beings who once again blew your flickering life into a new flame. Remember them with a full heart and profound gratitude.

Christmas Corruption

It is Christmas Eve, in the silent hours of the morning. My mind flows with a myriad of impressions. Tonight will be my favorite worship service of the entire year, the service at 11 p.m. with only candles to light the sanctuary. Eyes become moist — as midnight arrives — with chimes ringing and all singing *Silent Night, Holy Night.*

But I have other thoughts on this special morning, thoughts having to do with the one they called Jesus. What would he think of the obscene circus going on in America today in his name — the corruption of everything that he represented being so blatantly profane?

Maybe he hears again the words of God through Isaiah: "Bring me no more vain offerings, the sabbath and the calling of your assemblies, my soul hates."

What do I mean by the corruption of his name? On my desk is a Gannett News Service story, listing all of the Jesus gifts that were available for Christmas. In case you missed it, and you are spiritually sensitive, you may want to take two aspirin before you read further.

The first item was The Lord's Supper Talking Clock, with a drawing of the Last Supper on the face. Where Jesus sits there is a digital display of the time.

Now, are you ready for this? Are you sitting down? A different disciple announces the time each hour: "I am Peter, the time is now 12 o'clock—...." It may take more than two aspirin to recover from that.

Again, why do I say corruption of his name? A statement by New Right leader Paul Weyrich says it all: "We want to govern America."

At no time did Jesus want to govern anything. He was adamant in demanding a separation of church and state. Caesar and God were two separate considerations. Jesus set himself against a fanatical nationalism. He disclaimed a kingship, which was related to political power.

Jesus never participated in any political party. He never marched in the street for a social cause. He never camped out on the lawn and announced to reporters that he was now about to fast for pro-life or any other cause.

And there were causes in his day. There was murder, bigotry and prostitution. There were rich and poor, corruption and evil. There was child and spouse abuse, adultery, polygamy and divorce. (One of the women that Jesus was most tender with was the one at the well who had lived with five husbands and was then living with a sixth man — not her husband, a "significant other.") There was slavery and there were beggars, and yet Jesus never attempted civil reform, or went off into tirades against other nations.

He never made up a hit list of senators and congressmen, and he never promoted book burning or censorship. He never tried to create lobbying groups. Most important of all, perhaps, he never tried to force, coerce, threaten or intimidate people into following him.

The religious and political right today specializes in all of the above — all antithetical to the man of Nazareth, the man they say they are following. What a corruption of his name, his mission and his purpose.

"Once every hundred years, the gentle Jesus of Nazareth meets the dogmatic, militant Jesus of the Christian right in a garden. They visit for a while, and the end of the conversation is always the same. The gentle Jesus of Nazareth says to the militant Jesus of the Christian church, 'Oh my, we will never, never agree.'" (Paraphrased from Gibran's *Jesus*.)

I think — just maybe, someday, at some point — the dogmatic and militant Christian "right" truly will be born again and will begin to represent Jesus of Nazareth.

And then, just perhaps, the day will have arrived "when not a sparrow falls to the ground unknown . . . and the least shall be considered side by side with the greatest."

A Christmas Party
for Jesus

Once again, we are about to have a birthday party for a person named Jesus. As we approach the date, December 25, the same thoughts return to haunt me — thoughts that have played across my mind for years.

Babies are sweet and inoffensive. If we can just keep Jesus in a crib, which we do, there will be no problem. But if we celebrate the birthday of a man, there is a real problem, a problem that has to do with honesty, with truthfulness. If Jesus the man, who became a "great offense" *(Mark 6)* gave a birthday party in Boise — or any other city in America — the simple truth is that not one of us would go. Jesus would be left alone.

The clergy would certainly not attend the party for this wild, harsh and brazen man, with his scathing words for them: "The tax collectors and the prostitutes will go into the Kingdom of Heaven before you." *(Matthew: 21)*

He would cut through the legalistic Christian doctrines of today, saying once again "in vain do you worship me, teaching as doctrines the traditions and rules of men. You have a fine way of rejecting God in order to keep your traditions." *(Mark: 7)* The clergy would not be at that party.

The hawks and the military mentalities would not be there. They would call him a cowardly dove and pacifist, because he said to them "resist not evil." What a fool, our hawks say, "Has he never heard of that 'evil empire?'" But Jesus continues: "Turn the other cheek . . . He who lives by the sword will die by the sword . . . and love your enemies."

The business people, stockbrokers and Wall Street yuppies already would have scratched him off as a real nut for saying, "Take no thought for tomorrow, what you shall eat or drink, or what you shall wear." Geez, what was with him? Thinking about what to eat and wear is what keeps Christmas going.

Home lovers and counselors would not attend the party. Ask them why and they would say, "Did you hear what that screwball said to us? He said, 'If anyone does not hate his own father and mother and wife and children and brothers and sisters he cannot be my disciple." "'Hate,' he said . . . hate his family. Can you believe this guy?" *(Luke: 14)*

The Woman's Christian Temperance Union would not come to the party, because Jesus would be serving real, genuine, honest-to-God wine. He never heard of grape juice.

The thin-lipped pious and the squint-eyed moralists would not come close to this man who was called "a drunkard, a glutton and a friend of sinners" *(Luke: 7)*, who showed love for a prostitute, Mary Magdalene, and tender affection for an adultress and a woman who had lived with five husbands, and was now living with a man not her husband.

The wealthy would not attend the party of a man who told them: "It will be easier for a camel to go through the eye of a needle than for a rich man to enter the Kingdom of God." *(Matthew: 19)*

There is to be a birthday party on Dec. 25. Who would be there if that man still was there, still saying such offensive things?

It is Christmas Eve now in churches all across this land. Jesus begins to talk as he did 2,000 years ago. The ushers are becoming nervous; they can't believe what they're hearing. The faces of the clergy are flushed.

What to do? Why is this man ruining our sweet, perfumed worship service of fantasy. The choirs are getting up now to leave; they have had enough. The congregations begin to murmur, "This man must be insane. What are we doing here? Why doesn't he just stop talking, just shut up so we can go back to singing our sweet carols?"

But the voice continues as Christians pour out of the sanctuary, disgusted, headed for home. And the voice continues.

The Roman Catholic cathedral is now empty. The candles are out in the empty Protestant sanctuaries. The Christian churches all are dark. The only sound is snow, softly falling outside, and inside Jesus is left alone — with God.

Christmas Myth,
Legend and Folklore

We are buried this time of year in mythology, legend and folklore. It's good to get it all in perspective by rediscovering a few historical facts.

I have lost count of the thousands of times that we have been told that Christmas celebrates the origin of Christianity — which, of course, is false. Christmas was around for eons before Jesus was born.

The winter solstice (Dec. 22 to 25) has been celebrated for thousands of years. Solstice comes from two ancient words, sol, the name of a sun god, and stice, meaning still, or the day that the sun stands still, the shortest day of the year.

Since all cultures have been so dependent upon the seasons, the four major festivals centered on the summer and winter soltices and the spring and autumn equinoxes. An equinox — equi, meaning equal, and nox, meaning nights, or equal nights — occurs midway between the winter and summer solstice, when days and nights are equal in length.

Those are the four corners of the celestial year. But with the return of the sun to once again warm the earth and bring forth a resurrection of life, the winter solstice became the greatest of all the festivals.

The ancient festival in Rome was known as the Saturnalia. The emperor Aurelian established an official holiday called "Sol Invicti," meaning "unconquered sun" in honor of the sun god, Sol. It was held Dec. 24 and 25 and established Dec. 25 as the official solstice. All the other religions that worshipped sun gods also took Dec. 25 as their fixed date for their festivals.

A major one was in honor of the Egyptian divine mother, Isis. Early Christians used to worship in front of statues of Isis suckling her divine child, Horus, the babe that she had conceived miraculously. In 350, Pope Julius I decreed that the birth of Jesus would be celebrated on the same day as all the other sun gods, Dec. 25.

Other major birthdays celebrated Dec. 25 included those of the gods Marduk, Osiris, Horus, Isis, Mithra, Saturn, Sol, Apollo, Serapis and Huitzilopochli.

One of the more interesting myths — obviously related to the Christian myth — is that of Mithra. Mithra went to heaven until he returned a savior for all of mankind. A star fell from the sky when Mithra was born, shepherds witnessed the birth and Zoroastrian priests, called "Magi," followed the star to worship him. They brought golden crowns to their newborn "King of Kings." His birth was celebrated on Dec. 25. It was called the Mithrakana.

Now, when someone tells you that we just have to get back to the "true" meaning of Christmas, remember that the true meaning of Christmas is a celebration of nature, the sun and a return of the sun to warm the earth for resurrection and new growth. This has been the major festival in the life of human beings for at least 6,000 years — and quite possibly the last 15,000 to 20,000 years.

Christmas started at the formation of our solar system with our little planet — the third one out from a minor star named Sol — spinning on an axis that is tilted at a slight angle to its orbital path around the sun.

I like knowing where our celebrations fit into the large picture of our human family.

It relates me to "time past and time future . . . where past and future are gathered . . . pointing to one end . . . which is always present." (T. S. Eliot)

Christmas Music

My wife thinks I have a strange habit. Since about Nov. 1, she often has found me playing Christmas carols on my stereo when she comes into my study at home.

I might be playing the magnificent Mormon Tabernacle Choir, or *Christmas with Placido Domingo*, or *Barbara Streisand, A Christmas Album*.

My wife thinks that I start the season a little early. Imagine! But I thoroughly enjoy working with those nostalgic sounds in the background, and that brings me to the glory of music.

Dr. Lewis Thomas is writing today as beautifully as Loren Eiseley did in his prime. Thomas is a medical doctor and a research scientist in biology. Your mind will be stretched by reading any of his wonderful books. In *The Medusa and the Snail* he writes these words about music:

"Instead of using what we can guess at about the nature of thought to explain the nature of music, start over again. *Begin with Music* and see what this can tell us about the sensation of thinking. Music is the effort we make to explain to ourselves how our brains work. We listen to Bach transfixed because this is listening to a human mind. If you want to hear the whole mind working, all at once, put on *The St. Matthew's Passion* and turn the volume up all the way."

We know that rhythm came before melody, since rhythm alone is capable of satisfying both the emotional and the intellectual instincts of human beings, and remains so even today. A Buddy Rich can hold hundreds spellbound for long periods with nothing but the rhythm of a drum solo. The origins of rhythm are unknown, but the beat probably began with hand against hand, clapping, or the hand slapping methodically against the chest, as gorillas still do. Religious music began somewhere along our evolutionary path. It could have been 50,000 years ago or 75,000, but there is no doubt that primal people attached a definite religious significance not only to sounds themselves but also to the magical religious values they represented. The favor of the gods was obtained through ritualistic celebrations of rhythm, melody and dance.

There came a time when, as it reads in the Book of *Genesis*, "the sons of God came down off the mountains to the daughters of men and bore children to them. These were the mighty men of renown."

And so there came such a man, who surely seemed to have been sired by a God. His name: Johann Sebastian Bach, spiritual mystic, emotional poet, tone painter, romanticist. His magnificent *St. Matthew's Passion* has been called a work so intense, so deeply impassioned, so dramatic that it seems embroidered with tears and colored with flames and the blood. It still speaks to us today with unaltered eloquence and power.

From Neanderthal times, or Cro Magnon, making their rhythms, to Bach to Duke Ellington playing his famous mass in San Francisco's Grace Cathedral, God has been praised.

The sounds of music are everywhere: nights when the wind howls . . . the song of birds . . . the buzzing of insects and the murmuring of trees . . . fireside sounds or a creaking door . . . crickets chirping . . . a cat purring. All that is, is music. It needs only to be heard.

Music is the language of the spirit and the eternal speaks to us through this language.

May joyful sounds and strains fill your heart and home in this season. And yes, I am sure that I will start playing Christmas carols again next year, maybe even in October. My wife is getting used to it.

Christmas and 'Progress?'

In this Christmas season we are faced with a stark reality; the failure of so-called "progress" in all of its economic, technological and political applications, with an accompanying disillusionment. The British journalist-philosopher Malcolm Muggeridge expressed it well:

"It is deliriously funny, of course, going to the moon when you can't walk with safety through Central Park, or Hyde Park nowadays, after dark; fixing up a middle-aged dentist with a new heart in one part of Africa while in another part tens of thousands die of starvation in a squalid tribal war for which we, among others, provide arms; promoting happiness enriched by an ever-rising Gross National Product, and sanctified by birth pills and drugs for all on the National Health, while the psychiatric wards fill to overflowing, suicides multiply and crimes of violence increase year by year."

The anthropologist, Renaissance-man Loren Eiseley made a similar observation as to this stark reality when he held the chair of Philosopher of Science at the University of Pennsylvania: "The only sign of health remaining in man is the fact that he is still capable of creeping out of his thickening crust of scientific accomplishment to gaze around him with a sense of unease. We must replace our interests, our values and our priorities.

"Any future worth contemplating will not ever be achieved by flights to the moon, or outer space. It will be achieved only in the individual heart and mind of man as he contemplates beauty, justice, wisdom and truth.

"Without *spiritual insight*; without the ability to rise above scientific and mechanical expression, man will be consumed by a monster in his own brain."

In this Christmas season may our prayer be that humankind rediscover spiritual insight beginning with a penetrating look at our own souls and our own house. Is it not true that Jesus and Lao Tzu, the Buddha and Plato, Goethe and Albert Schweitzer, Thomas Jefferson and Carl Jung, T.S. Eliot, Robinson Jeffers and e.e. cummings, have far, far more to say to us than all of the bulletins coming out of Cape Canaveral?

Spiritual insight presupposes that the questions are asked, "What is man?" and "What is woman?" Who and what are we? I ask you the question now, "What are you?" A bundle of carbon, a walking calcium deposit? I can assure you that it is not hydrogen typing these keys, nor is carbon reading. Iron does not laugh; hydrogen does not cry; sodium does not love; oxygen does not pray; zinc did not write the *Messiah*. Where are *you* in that maze of pipes and protoplasm and chemicals? Whence came this spirit, this unseen "God within," that cannot be ex-

131

plained by neurology, chemistry, physics, physiology or biology? Whence came this spirit . . . out of what ancient cloudburst . . . what steaming pool?

If our prayer in this season is for a recovery of spiritual insight then we must begin by becoming conscious of who and what we are as a species and then transforming our attitudes, our daily lives and decisions, in all areas from political to economic, to be in harmony with that new vision.

In this season we are remembering one who tried to rekindle that vision in his own time. The vision that we all are children of God, the eternal presence, the mystery; that we all, each and every one of us on this planet, live in and by the same spirit, closer to us than our breath.

This season reminds us of the great spiritual insights that Jesus rekindled, which cannot and have not changed throughout the ages, and have belonged to every religion; primarily that there is within us all that divine presence, the "ethos," the "God within." We need a new birth in our own consciousness of the presence of this "kingdom within" us all.

For this truly is an answer to the question of who and what we are as human beings. As we thirst for truth, the spirit within us shifts and widens and expands; the spirit is there, waiting to be brought forth and converted into a source of more light for the fulfillment of human destiny.

Let us once again point our lives in the direction of divinity. And as we reach out to the eternal mystery, our souls will be ignited, showering out, like a sparkler, from the infinite light; the same light that will illuminate our individual wake for future generations, however modest or however brilliant.

THOUGHTS ABOUT MYSTICISM

Defining Mysticism

I think of myself as being within the stream of Christian mysticism. Many letters have asked me to say more about mysticism and Christian mysticism. Here are some general observations.

Mysticism is the recovery of the now, of the immediate. It is the recovery of intuition, of feeling. Experiencing God has nothing to do with anything in the past or the future, it is now. Mysticism refuses to deify Reason or Rationalism, spelled with capital R's. It is Carl Jung writing in his autobiography that "reason and rationalism are the two major diseases of our time."

It is the brilliant scientist Julian Huxley writing that "we must repudiate our modern idolatry of science. Science is only the name for a particular system of knowledge and understanding acquired by particular methods. It must come to terms with other systems of knowledge acquired by other methods, the aesthetic and the intuitive, the subconscious, imaginative and visionary." Or in other words, the way of mysticism.

A common misunderstanding is that mysticism is related to the bizarre or the occult. William Ernest Hocking said it this way: "Mysticism is not to be associated with occultism or superstitution, nor with psychical research, nor with cults of vagueness, nor with a love of the mysterious for its own sake."

Experience is the key word in mysticism. Truth is revealed through experience, rather than through doctrine, dogma or creed. It is reliance on spiritual intuition and personal experience in the discovery of a wisdom that gives a new vision and an understanding of reality. It is the mystic William Blake writing: "To see a World in a Grain of Sand and a Heaven in a Wild Flower, Hold Infinity in the palm of your hand and Eternity in an hour."

Whether Christian, Hindu, Taoist, Buddhist or the American Indian, the mystical experience is the same. It was the experience of Lao Tzu, the old master of Taoism, Buddha, the Roman Catholic Meister Eckhart, and the Protestant Boehme. The words of Jesus "to have seen me is to have seen God," and again, "I and the father are one" is pure mysticism.

To the mystic eye, the many things of the universe, including you and me, are all God and divine. As a Zen Master put it: "To watch a child pouring milk into a glass is to see God pouring God into God." Or as the Roman Catholic Christian mystic Meister Eckhart said: "The eye by which I see God is the same as the eye by which God sees me. My eye and God's eye are one and the same." And again: "Seeking God is like riding on an ox looking for an ox to ride."

The bridge from dogma to reliance only on inner experience is a difficult one for many to cross. Dogma becomes believed. It is hypostatized, as many Protestants hypostatize the *Bible*, making it a supreme authority regardless of its hundreds of contradictions and thousands of illegitimate and contradictory interpretations. "The kingdom of God is within you," said Jesus. "Be a lamp unto yourselves," said Buddha. "I am nourished only at the Holy Breast, by the divine One, the Mother-Spirit (the Tao), absorption in Eternity. The Great Light," wrote the mystic Lao Tzu.

Carl Jung made the observation that, "The creative mystic has always been a thorn in the side of the dogmatic and creedal church, but it is to the mystic that we owe all that is best in religion and humanity." Our final word is from the distinguished American psychologist William James (1842-1910): "The true mystic has insight into depths of truth that are unplumbed by the discursive intellect."

"Something unknown is doing we don't know what."

— Sir Arthur Eddington

"Man has need of a mystical supplement of the soul, and he must force himself to acquire it promptly before it is too late. It is the duty of those who have the mission of being the spiritual guides of humanity to labour to awaken in it this supplement of the soul."

— Prince Louis De Broglie,
winner of the Nobel Prize
in PHYSICS, from his
THE MECHANISM
DEMANDS A MYSTICISM

No "Dualism" in Mysticism

To continue with the subject of mysticism:

First, we must rid ourselves of the dualism that infects so much of our orthodox religious views of the earth and the universe. Dualism constantly separates man and woman from God, nature from man and spirit from matter.

Several years ago a Zen master was lecturing at Stanford University. He opened his address by stepping up to the front of the stage, leaning toward the audience and saying: "Man against God, God against man; man against nature, nature against man; nature against God, God against nature; very, very funny religion."

Many still want to apply the word symbol God to something "out there" that is separate and distinct from us "down here" on this planet Earth. It is always God *and* something else . . . God *and* us . . . God *and* the creation . . . God *and* the Earth . . . God *and* the creatures. Like the word God was a symbol for some "it" "out there."

Opposed to this view is the recognition that the word God is a symbol for the oneness of everything. Everything is one with God and nothing is separate from God. The mystery is within us, and every leaf, every atom, every molecule, within all. The universe is a totality and an interelatedness of all things. For the cohesive mystery within that totality — we use the symbol God.

Today's physics and quantum mechanics confirm that the classifications of organic and inorganic, animate and inanimate are archaic and invalid. (Of course, Eastern religions and the North American Indian traditions have been saying that for centuries.)

The illustration used by a Zen master in my last column on mysticism perfectly reflects this understanding of reality: "To watch a child pouring milk into a glass is to watch God pouring God into God." It is the same mystery and the same reality within the child that is within the milk that is within the glass. It is an interrelatedness and a oneness. God ceases to be an object and becomes an experience.

In *The Dancing WuLi Masters, an Overview of the New Physics* author Gary Zukav makes this observation: "The conceptual framework of quantum mechanics, supported by massive volumes of experimental data, forces contemporary physicists to express themselves in a manner that sounds, even to the uninitiated, like the language of the mystics. Access to the physical world is through experience. The distinction between the 'in here' and the 'out there' no longer exists." I commend this book to you, as well as *The Tao of Physics* by F. Capra.

As Dr. Donald Andrews of Johns Hopkins University put it: "Every time you lift your finger, the farthest galaxy feels the impulse."

Or, as James Jeans wrote: "Modern physics has reduced the whole universe to waves, and nothing but waves."

All galaxies, stars, planets and human beings are manifestations of waves. I am still talking about the oneness, the interrelatedness of everything that is tied together by . . . the mystery that is known only through experience.

Mysticism is an attitude of mind, a particular orientation to the world around and within us, an insight into the nature of reality and truth, a recognition of the oneness of everything that can be experienced directly. It is a spiritual sense of intuition, it is not going off and sitting in a cave somewhere, for the great mystics have not withdrawn themselves from the business of life. Jesus, wandering in Galilee, Lao Tzu, in the mountains of China, to the mystic Henry David Thoreau writing: "If for a moment we make way with our petty and trivial selves and cease to be but as a crystal which reflects a ray . . . what shall we not reflect! What a universe will appear radiant around us."

Christian Mysticism

The Hebrew scholar Rabbi Barnett Joseph, in a lecture on "Aspects of Jewish Mysticism" made the statement that "the *Bible* is the world's greatest classic of mysticism."

The *Bible* is saturated with mysticism: Moses, the prophets, Jesus, Paul, the author of *John* all were mystics. Biblical and mystical are not antithetical terms. The Psalmist of the Old Testament declared, "You are gods . . . all of you." (The Hebrew word here for "gods" is "Elohim," which literally translates God.)

Space, of course, precludes documenting the thousands of passages from the Old Testament that are pure mysticism, but for those of you who may want to seriously pursue this subject, I suggest you read the great work by Gershom Scholem, *Major Trends in Jewish Mysticism*. The two major schools of Jewish mysticism were the Cabbalah (Kabbalah, Tradition), and the Hasidists (Chassidists) pious.

They wrote "there is no place empty of God," and the divine "being" is found in all of the ordinary things of everyday life (yes, including milk). The Hebrew mystical treatise *Sefer Yesira*, which could be as early as the second century B.C., regards all existing things as outflowings of God, who is not *external* to anything in the universe, and all multiplicity is but an expression of the *one unity*. All is ultimately one with the One, as the flame is one with the candle.

The New Testament is mysticism from beginning to the end. Buddhism and Christianity were both founded by mystics. Words attributed to Jesus have him quoting the psalmist in *John* 10:34, "I said, you are Gods."

When asked as to where was the Kingdom of Heaven, Jesus replied, "within you." The author of *John* has Jesus saying, "I and the Father are One," and "to have seen me is to have seen God," all pure mysticism. The Sermon on the Mount is all mysticism: "consider the lilies" . . . "take no thought" . . . "resist not evil." When Jesus was asked why he spoke in parables, he replied: "Because it is given to you to know the *mysteries*. . . ."

Knowledge of the "mysteries" is always a major, pervading theme in mysticism. If the kingdom of God is within, as Jesus said, then all of those millions who pray "thy Kingdom come" are asking for inward union with God in the true mystic's sense. Jesus was explicit that the "Kingdom" was "not here, not there," but "within" us all. "I said . . . you are gods."

St. Paul was not only a mystic himself but a teacher of mystical doctrine. Paul was familiar with Greek philosophy, as well as the mystery religions of Greece, and the mystical Essenes in Palestine. He combined all of these to throw himself totally into a mystic relationship with "the God within" and the "Christ" within. Paul followed the same, identical, mystical formulas of the mystery religions of Greece: 1) the sharing of a rite by which members were initiated into a community; 2) rites of baptism; 3) disclosure of the formula for salvation; 4) a vision of the diety; 5) *union* with the diety; 6) eating the sacred meal that effects communion with the diety. And Paul writes of a God who is "above all, and through all, and *in you all.*"

The Gospel of *John* has been called the classic study of a visionary mystic combined with imaginative poetry. He opens his Gospel with the mystic Logos, the Word: "In the beginning was the Word, and the Word was with God, and the Word was God. . . ."

Among mystics since the time of Heraclitus, Logos had meant the immanence of the higher Spirit in human life, the Divinity of the soul, the presence of God in our consciousness. The 17th chapter of the Gospel of *John* is a recreation of the final rites of the Greek mystery religions. It is as simple and true a statement of mysticism as any in the literature of the world. His Gospel has been called the "charter of Christian mysticism" by the scholar Hugo Rahner, professor of church history, University of Innsbruck, whose special field is early Christianity.

Again, for those of you who want to do any serious reading on this subject, I commend *The Mysteries* (papers from the Eranos Yearbooks, edited by Joseph Campbell, Princeton University Press, the Bollingen series); it is a compilation of 13 scholarly papers delivered at the annual Eranos meetings in Switzerland.

With its roots in the New Testament, Christian mysticism grew and spread down the ages. Theological and philosophical giants within the Christian church have been mystics, from the Roman Catholic Meister Eckhart to the Protestant Jacob Boehme.

I hope that this has introduced you to a profoundly vast dimension of Christianity.

138

Hebrew Mysticism

Dr. Stanley Dean, Professor of Psychiatry at the University of Miami, and editor of the book *Psychiatry and Mysticism* writes that: "The study of mysticism should be part of the curriculum of medical schools." He defines mysticism as "knowledge or awareness that reaches consciousness through channels other than those known to us at present."

One of the major movements in Judaism today is a return to Hebrew mysticism. I have chosen the following examples to indicate the strength and direction of this movement.

Rabbi David Teutsch, executive director of the Federation of Congregations, writes that "We are moving toward a new Judaism. It will have as classical a shape when viewed a thousand years from now as Biblical Judaism has now. A new, revitalized Jewish spirituality will emerge."

Robbi Lynn Gottlieb describes the movement as experiencing "a freedom to take religion (and Judiasm) out of its conventional forms and bring it back to the heart and soul of the earth." It is a desire to create a new spirituality and physical unity with this planet.

Traditional Jewish services have been turned around and pointed in a new direction. Instead of sitting in orderly pews, facing East toward Jerusalem and reading from standard prayer books, the participants sit in a circle. The rationale is that, since God is within each one of us, it is better to look at your friend when you pray than to imagine an ancient Holy Temple.

Liturgy and ritual have been invented and revitalized. As one rabbi put it, "we no longer have to say prayers that stick to the roof of our mouth."

There is more meditation on nature. A Passover is celebrated that has male-oriented references edited out and includes contemporary references. A new moon celebration each month is based on the kabbalistic women's celebration. It is a return to the message of the 18th century Hasidic master Ba'al Shem Tov who said that God was "to be found everywhere and in everything . . . rejoice in that revelation."

This renewed interest in Jewish spirituality and mysticism is perhaps best represented by Rabbi David Zeller. As a graduate psychologist he was — and is — a serious student of the work of Carl Jung.

He spent years studying and making contact with every major mystical tradition. He lived with the Hopi Indians, studied in India with mystics of that tradition and studied in Israel, exploring the roots of Jewish mysticism. He sees himself as a bridge between traditional Judaism and the new movement that is rediscovering the values of Hebrew mysticism.

"There is a profound volcano going on in the Jewish community, and in other religious communities, in which the spiritual and mystical elements have been leached out . . . by orthodox and traditional doctrines," said Rabbi Arthus Waskow.

What we have done, you see, is to make creeds out of the mystical insights of other individuals (Jesus, Paul, etc.) and then have gone even further by attempting to institutionalize their visions and revelations.

Traditions, orthodoxies, creeds, dogmas, doctrines come and go, become archaic and antiquated, have their day and cease to be. But with an individual's personal, subjective, sensing and experiencing the mystery that saturates the entire cosmos like a sponge, the feeling of oneness with the mystery will be as personal, as moving, as intense today and tomorrow as it was thousands of years ago.

And from these experiences come "knowledge and awareness that reaches consciousness through channels other than those known to us at the present time." The experience can occur in a cathedral or on an alpine meadow blanketed with wild asters and blue delphinium — or gliding with fresh powder, at one and in harmony with the mountain, the wind, trees, sky and all things.

The celebrated Zen master Suzuki once was asked what was the point of mysticism. He said that before he studied and understood Zen he saw mountains as mountains and water as water. When he had made some progress, he no longer saw mountains as mountains and water as water. But when he got to the heart of Zen, he again saw mountains as mountains and water as water.

A student then asked Suzuki what was the difference between the first time and the last time he saw mountains as mountains and water as water. "No difference at all," he said "except the second time you are walking about two feet off the ground."

GOD AND THE TAO ...
EAST AND WEST ...
HOW WE DIFFER

The Beauty of Dawn Hours

The majority of us need to pay more attention to the way we start each new day.

It can make all the difference as to how the rest of the day unfolds, whether on a high and noble plane, or a survival contest to be endured.

Starting the day with a morning televison news broadcast is a downer from dawn on. The announcer, or anchor person, greets us with a hearty and hale "Good morning America," or something similar, and then immediately starts to tell us dozens of reasons why it is not a good morning at all.

We are exposed to all of the gory and offensive details of a gang-rape in the Northeast; next we are told how many human beings have been mutilated to indicate the violence; next comes what murders have taken place in the United States, followed by what prisoners have escaped and shot their way through the countryside, and on it continues with our eyes glued to the screen while our stomachs are trying, vainly and desperately, to do something with the ham and eggs throughout all of this violence, terror and bloodshed. We then, perhaps, rush for the newspaper to read about it all over again.

I think, surely, there must be a better way to begin a new day. "This is the day which the Lord God hath made . . . let us *rejoice* and *be glad* in it." How many times, hundreds of times, have I said that to myself? I have lost count.

I had a friend who refused to turn the television on or read a newspaper until sometime later on in the afternoon. I learned a valuable lesson from that. It can make a remarkable difference in how the day progresses.

Many years ago I started reading biographies and autobiographies of great and noble men and women, whose own lives were centered and balanced, and who had made contributions far beyond the normal. I was intrigued by the fact that practically all of the them started each day in similar fashion, on a high and noble plane.

Thomas Jefferson wrote that he always arose at first light and walked to enjoy the "freshness of the new dawn."

Erasmus wrote: "the muses love the early morning, as that is the perfect time for thought and study."

J. Frank Dobie, the brilliant iconoclast of the University of Texas, wrote that he took his pre-dawn coffee with Montaigne or Plato and, quote: "Would not wilt the freshest part of the day with the banalities of the news, but would 'rather start with the rhythms of the natural day.'"

It was customary among the Plains Indians of North America for each individual to leave the teepee alone, in the pre-dawn, and go off to greet the sunrise with thanksgiving and prayer to Wakan, the Mystery.

Carl Jung writes of his living with some of the primal peoples of Africa and relates the manner in which they started the new day.

"Sunrise was the most sacred hour of the day. The people would raise their arms to the sun, just breaking over the horizon. The gesture meant: 'I offer God my living soul.' I too, joined them, drinking in this dawn glory with insatiable delight, in a timeless ecstasy."

It has long been my habit, going all the way back to college days to arise about 5 a.m. and enjoy the early morning hours. It is the most magnificent time of the day to walk, or to read works of a high and noble plane.

There is beauty, quiet, harmony, vision and tranquility. There is a peace that is quite beyond my ability to describe. The natural world, in this little part of the cosmos, is preparing to receive the life-giving rays of the morning sun. The juices of life are flowing. Roosters are announcing their presence. Oftentimes, geese are honking. In days of winter, first light reveals a rainbow of pinks and purples to snow-covered mountains.

First light in spring, fields of wild flowers bathed in natural auras; and in a showery morning of summer, wild grasses, dew-covered, in concert with the heady odors of moist earth. How good they are, the flowers and the grasses, how beautiful, even though they will shortly vanish.

No church hymn will ever lift your heart higher than the early morning chorus of the birds. You will never see any painting more spiritual than dawn breaking, whether over Idaho mountains, a Nebraska clover field or the waters of Puget Sound.

It is the time of day that can distinguish coarseness from a divine refinement. It is the time of day when a person can look deeply into himself, and see things and not be fooled. It is the time of day when your vision can be seen clearly and the direction of your energies comes into focus.

Values and priorities become sharper, issues more clear, right decisions more obvious and the day begins on a high and noble plane. You are in harmony with yourself and the world. You feel . . . you know . . . that it is so, that, truly, this is the day which God has made . . . a day for rejoicing . . . and for being glad . . . in it.

Christian Circus Invites
the Silence of Zen

The distinguished historian Arnold Toynbee made a fascinating observation before he died. He wrote that when historians of the future look at our period, they are going to find that the single most important historical event was the penetration of Eastern religions into the orthodox Christianity of America.

We might ask, "is such an infusion taking place?"

• Thirty years ago, if you wanted to study a sacred Eastern text, it would have been almost impossible to find one outside of a university library. Today, every small corner bookstore in the country is crammed with all of the material anyone could want on Taoism, Zen, Hinduism, Yoga, meditation, mysticism and related subjects.

• Tour companies advertise: "Explore the Beauty and Mystery of Zen . . . Three weeks in Japan. . . ."

• In classes at the University of Puget Sound, I always asked my students, at the end of the semester, to name the section that had meant the most to them. Invariably it was the section on Zen and Taoism. Specific courses in Eastern religions were always full to overflowing.

• Many scholars and ministers within the Christian tradition are studying with Zen Masters. The noted theologian Paul Tillich, of Harvard and Chicago University, wrote an excellent book a number of years ago presenting the thesis that Christianity is judged by the religions of the East. Many seminars are being held around the country bringing together Buddhist monks, Zen masters, Christian ministers, professors of religion and Jewish rabbis.

• Contemporary physics, (quantum physics) says that perceptions of reality found in Eastern thought are far more in harmony with what is known today about the world we live in than are the archaic cosmologies of the *Bible*.

• No other religion, in the entire 100,000-year history of religion, has become so splintered, fragmented and unidentifiable as the one we call Christianity. (Zen is Zen, period. But what is Christianity? Is it Christian Science, Seventh Day Adventist, Mormon, Pentecostal, Unitarian, Jehovah's Witness, Lutheran, Roman Catholic or television evangelism?)

• Among questioning people today, there is an increasing disenchantment with dogmatic doctrines and ecclesiastical authoritarianism.

If more and more people, young and old, are searching for inspiration and contemplative education and finding it in Eastern concepts, we might ask why. Could it be because today's Christianity has projected images of hay rides, bingo nights, skating parties and church building religion, combined with bigoted judgments as to who is going to be saved and who is the real 100-percent *Good Housekeeping* approved Christian?

So-called Christianity is drowning in words, arguments, apologetics, talk, defenses, ranting and raving sermons, theological bickering and chatter. Many people are finding blessed relief in the quiet of Eastern religions, which is phrased best in the thought of the Vedas of classical Hinduism: "O Thou . . . Thou . . . before Whom all words recoil. . . ."

The Absence of Absolutes

There are some basic themes that run through Zen and Taoism (pronounced dowism) that are in direct contrast to Zoroastrianism, Judaism, Christianity and Islamism.

One major difference is the concept of complementary opposites, or the relativity of opposites. In our orthodox Christian tradition, we like everything simple. We want to say, "This is good and that is bad, this is truth and that is falsehood."

In Zen and Taoism, they laugh at this approach to life and reality. They tell delightful stories to illustrate how absurd it is to seek absolutes in truth, or good and bad. One of my favorites: The horse of a Taoist ran away and a friend said: "Oh!, that's bad. Your horse has run away." The Taoist replied, "Who knows . . . whether it is good or bad?"

About a week later the horse returned with a herd of wild horses, and the friend said, "Oh, that's good, for now you have 24 horses." And the Taoist replied, "Who knows . . . whether it is good or bad?"

Later that week, the son of the Taoist tried to tame one of the wild horses, was thrown off and broke a leg. The friend said, "Oh, that's so bad. Your son has a broken leg." The Taoist replied, "Who knows . . . whether it is good or bad."

A short time later the military came around to enlist young men, but they did not take his son for he had a broken leg.

The friend said, "Oh, that's good . . . your son does not have to go to the army." The Taoist answered, "Who knows . . . whether it is good or bad?"

Well, you get the idea. This sequence goes on forever to illustrate that you can never know, in any absolute sense, at any given moment, whether something is going to be good or bad, true or false. If you look back at your own life, you know that this is so. I can look back at events, relationships, ideas that I thought were good. They turned out to be a disaster. Those I thought bad at the time turned out to be good.

Another one of my favorite stories: What's good or bad depends on whether you are a man, a frog or a mosquito. To the man, the frog is good because he can eat the frog, but the mosquito is bad because the mosquito can eat on the man. To the frog, the man is bad because the man will eat him, but the mosquito is good because he can eat the mosquito.

To the mosquito, the man is good because he can eat on the man, but the frog is bad because the frog will eat him. So, what's good or bad depends on whether you are a man, a frog or a mosquito.

The point: What's good or bad depends on whether you are a Democrat or a Republican, a Holy Roller or a Taoist, a Buddhist or a Jew, a Hindu or a Moslem.

One more story: The Taoist is on a bridge watching the fish swim in the water below. He says to his friend "My, the fish are joyful today."

His friend answers. "You're not a fish. You don't know that they are joyful today." The Taoist replied "Well . . . you are not I . . . so you don't know that I don't know how joyful the fish are today!"

What they are saying with these stories is: All values are relative to the mind that entertains them. The symbol for this recognition of complementary and relative opposites is the Tai Chi disk, the Yin-Yang circle. (It looks like the Safeway logo.)

Everything in the cosmos, they say, is composed of complementary opposites, never rigid or frozen, but constantly changing positions as in light and darkness. If you hovered in a helicopter over a mountain all day, you would watch, from first light to the end of the day, the light and darkness down on the mountain changing positions.

They tell us that what seems to be a right answer today, may be wrong tomorrow. That giant of American letters, Ralph Waldo Emerson said it well: "Nothing is secure . . . except life and the energizing spirit. No love can be bound by oath or convenant to secure it against a higher love. No truth, so sublime, but it may be trivial tomorrow in the light of new thought."

To See God . . . Look In a Mirror

The most profound difference between Zen/Taoism and orthodox Christianity lies in answer to the question "What do you mean by God?"

In orthodox Christianity, God is something "out there," apart from everything else. Orthodox Christians still speak of the *Bible* as being the word of God, as though God was some "it" apart from the creation, speaking through some man-made vehicle on Earth, with secretaries taking it all down in shorthand or on tape.

Zen/Taoists laugh at these absurdities. They would call them spiritually infantile. A recent article in *Focus* magazine, a Christian publication, explained why Zen/Taoist countries have almost totally rejected Christianity: "In the Oriental mind there is no conept of monotheism, of a God who is almighty in power, all knowing in wisdom. They live by situational ethics, or Yin-Yang. They find ludicrous the concept of being 'saved,'" Interesting article.

Hundreds of years before Jesus was born, the grand old master of Taoism, Lao-Tzu, born of a virgin (a universal myth found in almost all religions) left just one slim volume of writings, the *Tao Te Ching,* or The Way and Its Power. The word God is, like the Tao, just a linguistic symbol for the mystery, the one-ness of all that is.

The Tao is the rhythm of life, the womb from which all comes and to which all will return. It is the rhythm of the universe. They ask "Do you want to see the Tao (or God)? Watch a cucumber cucumbering. Look into a wood fire and see the sun's energy dancing, as captured by photosynthesis. Watch a hawk riding the wind. Look at a pile of dung or salmon coming home to spawn, or just look in the mirror."

For hundreds of years, Christian mysticism also has spoken of the lack of separation between the mystery, humans, and all that is. The Christian mystic also would say "Do you want to see God? Then look into a mirror." It's Jesus saying "To have seen me is to have seen God." Every human, every leaf, bird, cat, dog, rock and flea could say the same.

That brilliant giant of Christian mysticism, Meister Eckhart, (1260-1329) wrote: "The highest angel and the fly are equal. All things are one, in God, and equal, a flea and the highest angel." And again: "He who knows the stones and the creatures would have no need to ever again listen to a sermon."

Or: "God is the fire of the hearth and the stable, as much as in devotion and rapture . . . wherever I am, God is, for the eye in which I see God is the same eye in which God sees me . . . for my eye and God's eye are One Eye. . . .

147

"Those who say they love God do not love him because he is 'good,' or 'eternal' or any such thing. On the contrary they love and enjoy God because they are God. . . .

"People say 'pray for me.' Then I think 'why do you always want to go outside of yourself? Stay within yourself, for you bear All The Truth There Is Within Yourself." So wrote that eloquent Christian.

A side thought: An interesting study is to compare the viciousness that exists within many Christian churches and groups with Zen/Taoist attitudes that would preclude such obscene behavior.

In Zen/Taoism and Christian mysticism, all is ONE. We share with every spark in the cosmos a oneness with the mystery. The energy that activates an electron is the same energy that brings a human being into fullness. Mineral, plant and animal, humans and the cosmos, we are all ONE, and all God.

Experience ...
NOT Dogma and Creed

Several years ago I made my fourth, and last, backpacking trip to the bottom of the Grand Canyon of Arizona. From now on I am going to let the mules carry me down that spectacular trail. It was one hike that I will never forget. It was the scene of one of the most moving, spiritual, experiences of my life.

I was alone, sitting on the sand beside the Colorado River. A slight breeze rustled cottonwood leaves, like an aeolian harp. Evening light faded into darkness and was soon replaced by a full moon, hovering, so near and immediate that I put out my hand and touched its face ... the face of God.

There was only time and the river singing. I could not possibly sleep. I was experiencing the origin of things. Rocks, close by, were over 3 billion years old. I was the only human and I was one with river, cottonwood, rocks, a full moon and the breeze.

I have lost count of the times that I have closed my eyes and relived that experience, an experience that moved my soul and my spirit to new depths of the eternal now. There is no way that I can share the depth of that experience with you through words. I can use the words cottonwood, river, wind, moon, and yet there is no word that I can use that can take you into that divine moment.

And here, at this point, we are at the heart of Zen and Taoism. They say, rightly, that experience completely transcends the reach of any language, and truth is always to be found through experience, and never from outside authority. What words do to us, they say, is to present a superficial world, an often phony world, a warmed over world.

Words can lead us into dead-end canyons, and what is the bottom line? It is this: Words fool us into thinking that we have experienced what we talk about.

Take water for instance: I can read volumes about water, go to study groups on water, listen to a thousand lectures on water and develop an exhaustive vocabulary about water, without having ever experienced water. I will know more about water after drinking a glass full, or diving into a lake than if I attend lectures on water for the rest of my life.

Take love: We say "Oh, I am such a loving person. I am constantly talking about love. I have read dozens of books on love. Why, I've told my kid a dozen times today ... "I love you honey," ... so see what a loving person I am."

You see the point? You can talk about love all day, for a dozen years, without having ever, genuinely, experienced love with a depth that causes your soul to burst with an overwhelming joy.

Now, take God: How many millions fool themselves into thinking that they have experienced God . . . because they are always talking . . . talking . . . forever and ever, talking, talking about God. They have read dozens of books about God . . . heard a thousand sermons about God, brown-bagged themselves to death in study groups about God. They say "why I got that Bible memorized. I can quote a thousand passages to you and talk forever about God. Of course, I know God."

As with water, this type of person will know more about God in five minutes, by just going out and sitting under the shade of a tree, listening to the flowers bloom, feeling the wind on skin, than by attending word-filled study groups about God for the rest of their lives.

As that giant of Christian saints, Meister Eckhart put it, "Once you have experienced the Indian paintbrush and the chipmunk, the rising full moon over the river and wind rustling cottonwood leaves (paraphrased) . . . you will never again have a need to listen to the hollow and parrot-like memorized . . . words . . . of a sermon. . . ."

The bridge from dogma to reliance only on inner experience is a difficult one for many to cross. Dogma becomes believed. It is hypostatized, as many hypostatize the Bible, making it a supreme authority regardless of its thousands of contradictions.

Truth is revealed through experience, rather than through doctrine, dogma and creed or the words of an ancient book. It is William Blake, writing "To see a World in a Grain of Sand and a Heaven in a Wild Flower, Hold Infinity in the palm of your hand and Eternity in an hour."

The Great Zen Master . . .
D.T., . . . Suzuki

The northern California and Oregon coast was simply glorious when my wife and I were there. I spoke to the Unitarian Fellowships of Sonoma County in Santa Rosa, California, and then we started north on the coastal highway with no itinerary, no plans, no telephones or television.

How can I describe the days? There were, as always, good books, the eternal ocean caressing white sands, the gentle breath of soft winds arriving from Japan and white puffs of cotton-candy clouds giving a third dimension to the blue beyond.

We fell in love with Mendocino, unpacked and stayed awhile. Our little cabin, just back from the ocean, riding a rocky ledge like an eagle's nest, was one with ocean, land and sky.

The words and thoughts that filled my spirit during those magnificent days were from *A Zen Life: Suzuki Remembered*, a tribute to one of the most beautiful men and Zen masters who ever lived. The contrast between the serenity, wholeness and beauty of his centered life, compared with the obscene and gross lives of the Jim Bakkers, Jimmy Swaggarts, Oral Roberts and others of like mentality was glaring.

The noted historian Arnold Toynbee wrote that the transfer of Buddhism, Zen and Taoism to the Christian West someday would be seen as one of the most significant events in history.

D. T. Suzuki played a major role in initiating that movement. His life finally moved on from this earth to other sacred dimensions in his 96th year. It was a life filled with the most brilliant scholarship and philosophical thought. People from across the spectrum of religions, vocations and nationalities wrote, in that book, that just to be in Suzuki's presence was a "never to be forgotten experience," an experience of such beauty that they broke down and wept upon leaving. Other observations from the book will give you a bit of the flavor and depth of the man:

• "He was the totally sound and complete man. He lived life as natural and as effortless as a flowing stream. He moved in the realm of complete freedom.

• "He was a man who thought with his whole body and mind, as one, and would not speak of what he did not know.

• "There was silence in his speech and speech in his silence.

• "He fully agreed with Carl Jung that with the exception of Christian mysticism there is nothing in traditional Western Christianity that approaches the profundity of Zen (or Taoism).

151

• "He lived in the now. I never saw him rushed or in a hurry. On the last day of a conference in Switzerland, everyone was rushing around to catch planes, trains, everyone by Suzuki that is. When asked why he was not preparing to leave, he replied "in two days there will be a full moon over Lake Zurich. I must stay to see it.'"

The truths, the themes, the concepts of reality that are to be found in Zen and Taoism have nothing to do with sitting in a cave contemplating your navel. But they have everything to do with how you approach your days and live your life, even in the busiest office in downtown Boise, Chicago or Seattle.

Zen tries to point you toward the sacred moment . . . the mystery that is ever present. Suzuki used these words to describe the experience: "Man is a thinking reed but his great works are done when he is not calculating and thinking. 'Childlikeness' has to be restored with long years of training in the art of self-forgetfulness. When this is attained, man thinks yet he does not think. He thinks like showers coming down from the sky; he thinks like the waves rolling on the ocean; he thinks like the stars illuminating the nightly heavens; he thinks like the green foliage shooting forth in the relaxing spring breeze. Indeed, he is the showers, the ocean, the stars, the foliage."

Zen tells you to awake to the miracle of this moment! There is glory in the commonplace, and much, much more.

Full Moon on Snow

There is a spiritual element to snow, expressed in Haiku. The Zen poet holds up a mirror and we see beauty, tranquility and spirituality:

"Fields and mountains . . . All taken by snow. There is neither heaven nor earth . . . only Snow . . . falling . . . under the winter moon."

There is also a spiritual element in skiing, in the wedding of human spirit and snow, when the body, mind, emotions, spirit and the elements unite to become one entity. And when they are united under a full moon, magic is present. Full moonlight and snow belong to one another.

I remember a good friend describing one of the most moving, spiritual experiences of his life. It was in January, about mid-night, the snow-covered earth sparkling under a dazzling full moon. Dormant feelings and energies surfaced. To remain indoors would have been impossible, under the magnetic pull of cosmic energies calling to his sleeping household.

My friend awakened his wife and children and told them to look out the windows and see this miracle of beauty. The entire family put on ski clothes and promptly went out into the night. For over an hour they skied, in what he called a perfect stillness.

The family, he said, would never again take the full moon and the snow for granted. They had experienced a living, spiritual miracle.

These thoughts came to me last week as I looked at my December calendar. The full moon falls today. And today, in West Yellowstone, Montana, is the first day of the U.S. Biathlon Olympic trials, which will last until Thursday. Our United States Olympic team will be chosen from this competition.

America's greatest Biathalon skiers will take part in this demanding encounter with snow and solitude — demanding of body, muscle, nerves, mind and spirit. There always has been a relationship between discipline and experiencing the Mystery, and there is no Olympic event more disciplined than the Biathlon.

It's fitting that the first day of the trials should also be the first day of the full moon, to celebrate the wedding of moon and snow. Under a full moon, snow and solitude provide the perfect setting for spiritual ecstacy.

I am a moon child, born under the sign of Cancer, the only one ruled by the moon. So maybe something deep within, coming from I know not where, is using my fingers to write these thoughts. But you don't have to be born under Cancer to feel the magnetic pull of the full moon and to stand in awe before the majesty, beauty and mystery of a full moon over snow.

153

Perhaps skiing offers the ultimate in experiencing this mystery. That superb author, Laurens Van Der Post, wrote a paragraph that I have never forgotten: "the spirit of man is nomad, his blood bedouin, and love is the aboriginal tracker on the faded desert spoor of his lost self; and so I came to live my life not by conscious plan or prearranged design but as someone following . . . the flight of a bird."

A Zen Day with Two Shih-Tzu's

It was a Zen day that my wife and I recently relished. In Zen they say that highest modes of spontaneous experience transcend the reach of any language. And so it was on that recent day.

We had checked off the last of our errands while in Boise and were ready to start back up the canyon to McCall. It was a breathless day of spring. It was high noon. There was a cloudless purity in the heavenly deep. The air was to be savored as if it were a fine glass of wine. It was a day to celebrate . . . the NOW of the eternal moment.

It was a day to remember that one of the most vital elements of life is festivity, the capacity for a genuine, joyous celebration of life; the sheer goodness of what is . . . the pure wonder and delight of being intensely alive, and aware.

We have such a relatively short time to wonder as we wander on this beautiful planet, and lest we forget, as e.e. cummings reminds us: "Since feeling is first, who pays any attention to the syntax of things, will never wholly kiss you, wholly to be a fool while spring is in the world, for life is not a paragraph, and death, I think, is no parenthesis. . . ."

It was the day before a new winery was to open. We thought, how perfect for the picnic lunch that we had in the car. It should be quiet and tranquil before the crowds arrived the following day. And so it turned out to be. Our picnic table was shortly graced with wine, cheese, apples and pocket bread. Earth odors of spring were heavy on a soft breeze. A sea of marigolds and geraniums were glorifying the beauty and the precision of the present moment. The sparkling little stream nearby had promptly drawn our two Shih-Tzu's like a magnet. They were now stretched out on their stomachs in the shallow water enjoying a pleasant conversation with a gardener nearby. Animals have no problems with festival and celebration. What teachers they can be for us, the "rational," and "logical" ones.

There are days, hours and moments such as this when you and mountains, rivers, trees, flowers, wind, water, soil, sky, moon, sun, rocks, wine and apples, cheese and pocket bread and dogs in a stream are all one and whole . . . "and the mountains and hills break forth into singing, and all the trees of the fields clap their hands. . . ." (*Isaiah 55:12*).

Cleansed in this experience of oneness, the words of Eihei Dogen came back to me through the quaking leaves: "This life of one day is a life to rejoice in. Because of this, if you can be awakened to the truth that the day is vastly superior to an eternal life, if this one day in the lifetime of a hundred years is lost, will you ever get your hands on it again?"

May I call to your attention, in case you have forgotten, even for a moment, the miracle of existence that is beyond comprehension. For we who have become so preoccupied with gaining and spending, winning and losing, spring is here and summer is coming. For how many will it come and go without a moment of astonishment, a day's amazement, or an hour's wonder at the miracle of it all?

Wonder is the capacity for sustained awe and joy. Wonder is a sense of freshness and spontaneity. Every day is a surprise party. Life is a cafeteria of delights, a new flower, a butterfly on the breeze, a hummingbird hovering, a cucumber cucumbering, a hug from someone loved, to sense the ultimate in the common, in the rush of the passing, the stillness of the eternal. . . .

"Earth is crammed with heaven, and every bush is afire with God, but only the person who sees, feels, hears and tastes takes off his shoes."

The Spirituality of Skiing

On a clear day, from the top of Brundage Mountain, you can see forever.

It must surely be as spectacular as any view in North America. It is 360 degree's of mountains, valleys, lakes and rivers. Even with my moderate ability on skis it is a spiritual experience. I do not use the word spiritual lightly. You can easily become one with the snow, sky, trees, floating clouds and the mountain.

I am not the first to call it a spiritual experience. The brilliant philosopher Martin Heidegger was offered prestigious teaching positions all over the world, but he chose to stay in his little Black Forest town of southwest Germany, teaching at the small university of Freiburg. He cherished his ski mountains and his little rustic cottage, Todtnauberg, that he built in 1928.

A *New York Times* article reporting his death referred to him as an "avid hiker and an expert skier well into his 80s, who liked to hold seminars with his students while skiing." Heidegger wrote of "the round dance of appropriation; the interrelationship of the fourfold: earth, sky, gods, and mortals. The skis bring together the united four, earth and sky, divinities and mortals."

On a sharp winter day, with every snow crystal glittering under sun rays, and every pine needle framed upon a mat of deep blue, silently the skier glides, flowing with gravity and becoming one with the mountain "receiving the sky and expecting the gods." There is freedom. There is grace and joy.

Heidegger looked upon it as an ultimate spiritual experience. he believed that we become authentic only as we live close to the earth and the natural rhythms, and stay in harmony with those same rhythms. He found the finest expression of this in skiing.

Tom Bender wrote about it: "In skiing, there is a line. It is a sacred line . . . the slalom . . . a line of moving, dynamic balance with the flows of energy in the place. There, for a few minutes, one can get close to the streamings of energy that are our universe."

The purpose of religion for thousands and thousands of years has been to put human life into direct contact with the life of the cosmos: mountain life, cloud life, sun life, moon life, water life, earth life, rain life, snow life, plant life, animal life, storm life, rock life and so receive energy, joy and transformation.

Krishnamurti said it this way: "Religion is living with an inward harmony, a feeling of total unity with the earth and the cosmos. Walking in the woods, silently, with the light of the setting sun on top of the mountains, or on a leaf, there is complete union between you and that.

There is no "you" at all. There is no "observer." There is no "fragmenta-tion."

We human beings are only a very small, minute part of a whole in-tegrated system. Perhaps skiing, as few other activities, brings us into an intimate relationship with that cosmic system, and a oneness with it. Now, what I have to do is improve my skiing enough to experience more fully what I know is there, waiting.

I was in my favorite ski shop the other day and was told that my present skis were too short, and therefore they would get nervous, with my weight and height. That did it! "Nervous" skis on "nervous" feet attached to a "nervous" body would be just too much for even the cosmic mystery to overcome. So I bought a new pair.

There is a trail on Brundage called the Boundary trail. Almost any-one can ski that. If you would like to experience the purest quiet and solitude, try it. My wife and I call it a spiritual path. There is only you, time, and the mountain flowing. There are birds, and wind whisper-ing through pine needles. There are brilliant snow-clad peaks and val-leys clothed in linen white to absorb. There is not one man-made sound. The mountain, the sky, the trees, snow, wind and you become one.

And I shall go down from this airy space, this swift white peace, this stinging exultation;

And time will close about me, and my soul stir to the rhythm of the daily round.

Yet, having known, life will not press so close, and always I shall feel time ravel thin about me;

For once I stood . . . in the white windy presence of eternity.

Eunice Tietjens

Still . . . the Dream

Traditional, orthodox and institutional religion is coming to the end of a 2,000-year cycle. There is a resurrection taking place: a resurrection of spirit (spirituality) from the tomb of this monopolistic and monomaniacal structure.

For 2,000 years the authoritative and dogmatic Christian church has supported conquest, materialism, exploitation, the rape of the Earth, hierarchy, political tyrannies, the demeaning of the sacred rituals and beliefs of primal peoples and our Native Americans, and the degradation of women. This phallic imperialism of the past 2,000 years is coming to an end. The institutional church has been, and is, a human political construction that is now in the throes of its own Ghost Dance. *The resurrection of 'spirit' from this dying monolith will turn out to be one of the most significant events in the history of civilization.* Millions are moving away from the dead forms and defunct symbols of the dogmas and doctrines of orthodoxy to the beauty of direct experience.

Leading this resurrection of spirituality out of the tombs of this establishment are the women who are rediscovering their orientation to the divine principle of the Goddess, this divine Goddess that we call Earth. This resurrection movement begins with a reaffirmation of the Earth as a living, breathing entity. Gaia, mother Earth, the sacred goddess, as the Greeks called her; Maka Wakan, the sacred earth, as the Native American Sioux thought of her. From the soil of this basic premise will flower the birth of spirit, a new consciousness, that includes, combines and makes whole as ONE, everything that is a part of this sacred Goddess: every four-legged and two-legged animal, every winged one of the sky and fish of the sea, every grass of a showery summer and flower of a rainy Spring, every grain of sand and drop of water, every rock, mineral and crystal, every leaf, bud and snowflake, all is ONE and all is divine and all offers thanksgiving to our great Mother Goddess, Earth, for her support and sustenance. A new consciousness, not any theological 'belief' is at the heart of this resurrection of spirituality.

A most remarkable conference was held in the late 1970's with Nobel Prize-winning physicists. The title was: *New Dimensions of Consciousness.* Their press release said this: "We are on the brink of a new synthesis, pioneered by visionary men and women, leading to a new consciousness."

Pictures of this great Goddess, Earth, as taken from the moon, triggered a shift in the collective psyche of millions. It was the spectacular view of Earth rising: a symbol of wholeness, a symbol of the mandala. Apollo 10 astronauts photographed the magnificent and awesome splendor of Earth . . . rising . . . above the horizon of the moon. EARTHRISE! What a breathtaking symbol of this new spiritual consciousness. There are no horizons in space, even as there must not be any horizons in our own spiritual experiences. After seeing EARTH-RISE above the horizon of the moon in those glorious photographs, we have seen with our own eyes that there is only ONE reality: that we are in the stars and we are in the heavens . . . that we ARE the stars . . . we ARE the heavens . . . NOW. We are being sustained by ONE Source . . . call it Spirit.

We are ONE with our Great Goddess, the sacred Earth, and we are ONE with the furthest star in the furthest galaxy. We sense, we feel, that somehow in some way, we all together are 'dancing to a whispered voice overheard by the soul.' Take that joy with you as you remember that the Great Goddess of nature creates and makes all things new.

Epilogue

Wordsworth used these words: "A sense sublime . . . of something far more deeply interfused . . . whose dwelling is the light of setting suns . . . and the round ocean and the living air . . . and the blue sky and the mind of man . . . a motion . . . and a . . . SPIRIT . . . that impels all thinking things . . . all objects of all thought . . . and rolls on through all things . . . ."

The great experiences of the human soul in beauty, love and intellectual illumination come to us again, and yet again, in sacred dimensions through a SPIRIT that is beyond human comprehension. That SPIRIT that sustains the universe . . . that SPIRIT that is the source of the trees, the flowers and the fruits . . . the very substance of the vegetables and the minerals . . . that SPIRIT that fills the sea with fish and the air with birds and the land with animals . . . that SPIRIT that is in the midst of me . . . continually enfolding and unfolding me . . . that SPIRIT that is the source of my supply and the very food upon my table . . . that SPIRIT that is closer to me than breathing . . . and so whither shall we go from this SPIRIT . . . and whither shall we flee from its presence . . . . What name shall we give it . . . this SPIRIT . . . it needs no name . . . other than Mystery . . . .

To leave this Mystery unknown and unnamed is not to lose . . . for silence names as well as sound . . . and it is enough . . . to remember that this SPIRIT . . . .

"In the blush of every dawn . . . in the evening breeze . . . in the leaf's low murmur . . . the swell of the ocean and seas . . . the rising and ebbing of the tide . . . the mote in the sunbeam . . . rest here, I whisper to the atom. I call to the orb . . . roll on. I am what was . . . is shall be . . . creations ascent and fall . . . the link . . . the chain of existence, beginning and end of all. Artist of the solar spaces . . . and of human faces . . . though all human races claim Thee . . . thought . . . and language fail to name Thee . . . mortal lips are dumb before Thee . . . Silence, only, can adore Thee . . . ."

O Thou . . . Spirit . . . thou . . . before whom all words recoil . . . .